ST. MARY PARISH LIBRARY

3 3446 00738 7901

158.1   Berg, Karen (Karen E.)
BER   Your self-sabotage   *uide*:
3/16/15 survival guide   AME

"*Your Self-Sabotage Survival Guide* is a well-packed* em that offers inspiration to both early starters and individuals who need to re-connect with courage and hope. The book skillfully weaves self-reflective narratives of respected mentors spanning multiple disciplines with a systematic exploration of presentation, growth, and transformation."
—Peregrine M. Kavros, PhD, MBA, clinical instructor, program in human sexuality, department of psychiatry, New York University School of Medicine

"*Your Self-Sabotage Survival Guide* is an essential tool for creating and sustaining success in all your endeavors. Karen Berg's words will inspire and guide your path through life. She writes with passion and compassion about the challenges we all face and how to overcome them."
—Robert Maurer PhD, director of Behavioral Sciences, Family Practice Residency Program at Santa Monica UCLA Medical Center. Author, *The Spirit of Kaizen*

"As a theatre journalist, I have observed highly talented people sabotage their gifts. Berg's book offers the kind of life-changing strategies that could save a career."
—Retta Blaney is the author of *Working on the Inside: The Spiritual Life Through the Eyes of Actors*

D0367633

ST. MARY PARISH LIBRARY
FRANKLIN, LOUISIANA

ST. MARY PARISH LIBRARY
FRANKLIN, LOUISIANA

Your Self-Sabotage Survival Guide

How to Go From Why Me? to Why Not?

By Karen Berg

THE CAREER PRESS, INC.
Pompton Plains, NJ

Copyright © 2015 by Karen Berg

All rights reserved under the Pan-American and International Copyright Conventions. This book may not be reproduced, in whole or in part, in any form or by any means electronic or mechanical, including photocopying, recording, or by any information storage and retrieval system now known or hereafter invented, without written permission from the publisher, The Career Press.

YOUR SELF-SABOTAGE SURVIVAL GUIDE
EDITED BY ROGER SHEETY
TYPESET BY DIANA GHAZZAWI
Cover design by Ty Nowicki
Printed in the U.S.A.

To order this title, please call toll-free 1-800-CAREER-1 (NJ and Canada: 201-848-0310) to order using VISA or MasterCard, or for further information on books from Career Press.

The Career Press, Inc.
220 West Parkway, Unit 12
Pompton Plains, NJ 07444
www.careerpress.com

Library of Congress Cataloging-in-Publication Data
Harzog, Beverly Blair.
 The debt escape plan : how to free yourself from credit card balances, boost your credit score, and live debt-free / by Beverly Harzog.
    pages cm
Includes index.
 ISBN 978-1-60163-360-6 -- ISBN 978-1-60163-392-7 (ebook) 1. Finance, Personal.
2. Consumer credit. 3. Debt. I. Title.

HG179.H3188 2015
332.024'02--dc23

2014045679

In memory of Alex.

This book is dedicated to my friends, family, clients, and colleagues who have stuck with me through thick and thin. You make my life the exciting journey I live for everyday.

▶▶▶▶▶▶▶▶▶▶▶ ◀◀◀◀◀◀◀◀◀◀◀◀◀

A huge shout out to Francine LaSala, who has been the angel on my shoulder throughout the birthing of the book. Thank you for your talent, humor, patience, and encouragement every step of the way.

Thank you to Career Press for once again believing in me. A special thanks to Adam Schwartz, Michael Pye, Laurie Kelly-Pye, Kirsten Dalley, Gina Schenck, and Allison Olson. What a team!

And none of this would have happened without my wonderful agent, Sharon Bowers, who continues to trust that I will deliver.

A note of thanks to Dawn Butcher, Judd Cady, Dr. Paul Hershenson, Mary Anne Prevost, Agnieszka Radecka-Zaniewski, and Yesenia Pedraza, each for your unique contribution.

A special thank you is reserved for Phil Hall, who never ceases to amaze me with his insights, imagination, intelligence, talent, and ability to see the "funny" of life, and who inspires me every minute of every day.

And speaking of inspiration, a huge thank you to all the professionals who gave their precious time and advice for "Words From the Wise" and "Why Not" sections of my book: Richard Armstrong, MD; Richard Berg; Tom Blakey; Laureen Cook; Douglas DeMarco; Robert Diamond; Karl duHoffmann; Melissa Errico; John Frazier; John Foreyt, PhD; Lana Gersman; James Gerth; Byron Gilliam; Phil Hall; Sharon Halley; Grant Herman; Catherine Hickland; Laurence Julliard; Lee Koenigsberg; Angelo Lambrou; Cheryl A. Marshall, PsyD; Bud Martin; Michael Mastro;

Katherine Mastrota, OD; Alan Matarasso, MD; Deborah McCarthy; Kevin B. McGlynn; Andre Mechaly; Jeremy Merrifield; Ricardo Morales; Linda Moshier; Julia Murney; Riley Nelson; Chuck Pineda, Karen Radwin; Ron Raines; Cheryl Raymond; Gee Rittenhouse, PhD; Cathy Russell; Martin Samual; Michael James Scott; Rob Sedgwick; Parinaz Sekechi; Samantha Stroh Bailey; Art Stevens; Merri Sugarman; Karla Visconti; Phong Vu; Scott Warren; and Jeff Winton.

Contents

Introduction

"What doesn't grow, dies." Everyone knows this. And yet, when it comes to our own potential, we somehow seem to forget all about it. We stifle ourselves. We sabotage ourselves. And as a result, we get nowhere.

Do you feel like the proverbial hamster in a wheel? Do you feel like no one notices you or any of your efforts? Do you feel like the world is letting you down, not presenting the right opportunities for you to seize?

Well, sorry to break this to you, but the world is not the problem. The problem is you. You're not getting ahead because you're standing in your own way. No one can see what you truly have to offer because you're actually blocking yourself. But that the problem is you is actually a very good thing, because you and your behavior and actions are the only things in this world you do have control over.

It's time to take back your dignity. We have felt suppressed, abused, and exploited in the marketplace for too long. It's time to rise up and take action, but take action appropriately. This is the era to let your voice shine through, but it must be in such a way that persuades others to embrace your attitude, not be terrified of it. People are angry, feel betrayed, let anger fester, and then explode in ways that are harmful to their colleagues and themselves. With this book, I'm going to show you how to get back on top and do it the right way!

You bought this book for a reason. You want to succeed. Great! Now it's time to work on you. It's time to modify your behavior and maximize your actions. It's time to stop sabotaging yourself and start succeeding, to re-plot your course and reinvent your existence. This book will help you to refocus your energy and get back on track with clear strategies for stopping self-sabotage. It will help you get rid of the "buts," banish the "if onlys," and help you to break the cycle of "playing it safe."

I've spent the past 30 years both reinventing myself and helping clients find their own mojo at various stages of their career. I've worked with colleagues and friends when they have lost their passion and have needed a jump start, when they have stalled either by self-sabotage or by their employer's change of game plan. So not all sabotage is your fault, but you can apply the strategies you will learn here to reinvent yourself even if the sabotage that brought you here wasn't technically your doing.

With this book, I'll show you how to walk into a room and light it up instead of draining it dry. I'll coach you on how to make people want to fall in line behind you, listen to you, and relate to you. I'll give you exercises, techniques, and strategies that will help you to see how you've gone off course and get you back on the right path.

I'll also introduce you to some strategic risk takers from a wide range of industries and from all age groups. I have included thought leaders from the corporate world and the entertainment community because I straddle both worlds and I have seen firsthand what each of these universes has to offer the other. As I say throughout this book, "There's no business like show business, and all business is show." It's amazing how much overlap there is between them.

I've chosen my panel of experts because I have either worked with them or have deeply admired their work. These leaders will share stories about their experiences with self-sabotage, either their own or from people they have managed. They'll provide tips on navigating away from self-sabotage. Some will even share their own reinvention "Why not?" stories, which are sure to stir and inspire you and help you become revitalized, focused, and self-confident, no matter what age you are.

It's time for you to go from "Why me?" to "Why not?" It's time for you to stop self-sabotage and to reinvent yourself to finally get the success you deserve—because you worked for it.

PART 1

ELEMENTS OF SABOTAGE

There's no business like show business—and all business is "show."

It doesn't matter if you're a lawyer or a graphic designer or a maître d'. As Shakespeare said, "All the world's a stage, and all the men and women merely players." For performers, it's essential to give a good "show," but it matters for all of us. Most of us forget that; we forget to be aware of ourselves, and that's where sabotage starts to creep in and take over.

We have to be as aware of ourselves and our actions as actors are at auditions. Everything we do needs to be treated like we're determined to clinch that big role. In this day and age, we're "on" all the time. All eyes are on you, to achieve or fail. That's why you need to set your mind on achieving and work at it every day—except we don't do that. Instead, we allow ourselves to be carried through our careers on the backs of bad behaviors. As a result, we don't get anywhere.

It's time to turn that around—first by awareness and then by action.

Get yourself a fresh new journal to use for this book and keep it handy as you read. The journal will become your own personal chronicle of how you overcame sabotage, and will make a great reference if you ever begin to slip back into the clutches of self-sabotage.

In this short section, I'm going to outline some of the many ways people sabotage themselves professionally and personally, and help you discover which sabotaging behaviors you may be guilty of. In the next section, we'll work to fix them.

Let's go!

1

Your Biggest Obstacle: YOU!

It had long since come to my attention that people of accomplishment rarely sat back and let things happen to them. They went out and happened to things.
—Leonardo da Vinci

Are you not getting ahead in your life and career due to any of the following situations or reasons?

"I was born to the wrong family."

"My parents didn't push me when I was growing up. That's why I can't get ahead."

"I was born in the wrong era."

"I wish I had time to take a professional enrichment class."

"My boss doesn't understand me."

"I had all the right qualifications for the job. I guess they didn't like me."

"I was told I would receive some help to finish my project, but I haven't received any."

If you're sabotaging yourself, you're not alone. Self-sabotage is an epidemic. In my experience, roughly 85 percent of people sabotage themselves.

Self-sabotage is insidious, profound, and universal. Many of us walk around engaging in negative behaviors and mindsets, and we don't even realize we're doing it. Every day, people from all industries are working hard to get nowhere. This is because in every single sector, from education to entertainment, from medicine to marketing, people—smart, highly educated people—sabotage themselves by not being in the moment, by letting their thoughts spiral out of control in business meetings, and by drifting away from the point. Not to mention the havoc they wreak on their professional persona with their social media footprint! Did you know that even your doctor Googles you these days? You have to be careful what you're putting up there in social media—and yet, people aren't.

Even top-level executives sabotage themselves. Here's a recent example that comes to mind.

Paul and his team were a group of high-level executives that had been given a chance to make a huge deal with a corporation based in Africa. If they made the deal, it would be a crowning achievement for their group and a giant coup for their company. Needless to say, they took the job very seriously. They worked nights and weekends getting ready. Paul missed a big family reunion, while other members of his team ducked out of various soccer games and date nights. Paul's second-in-command, Regina, even missed attending a wedding.

They labored for weeks preparing the PowerPoint and perfecting their presentation. Because these were top-level folks, they understood that the international language of business is typically English, so they prepared their entire presentation in English. Like machines or robots, they never once questioned whether the language they were going to be presenting in was the correct language for their client; they just robot-ed forward.

At last, the work was done and it was the team's time to shine; they were loaded with confidence. They landed in Africa a full 24 hours before the big meeting to get proper rest, go over their presentation, and make sure the room they were presenting in could accommodate their tools.

Finally, the meeting time arrived, and the team geared up to greet the client. But as soon as the head of the group entered the room and greeted Paul with a warm "*Bonjour*," Paul's heart sank into his shoes. For all his team had been on top of, they missed one crucial detail: the country they were to be presenting in used French as their go-to business language, not English.

After all that time preparing, not to mention the thousands of miles they traveled, they were thrown out of the conference room. After all that work, they didn't even have a chance to present, let alone make the deal, all because no one thought to break out of the routine and learn more about the country they'd be presenting in. They all just went about their busy work, not considering the world beyond their spreadsheets and PowerPoint slides.

▶▶

Words From the Wise—Deborah McCarthy
Director, Results Delivery Organization, Alcatel-Lucent

It's Up to Me

Here are some aspects of self-sabotage I witnessed in my career.

- ▶ *Faking who you are*: I always try to be true to myself and genuine in my dealings. One of the factors that contributes to self-sabotage is being someone you're not and saying things that are simply not your own. It is impossible to defend or sustain being something I am not. I don't even try. In the long run, it leads to failure and disappointment, both for myself and the people who depend and believe in me.

- ▶ *Doing things for the wrong reasons*: Always do the right thing for the right reasons. I cannot let my "personal" agenda get ahead or be more important to what I do and who I support.

- ▶ *Not "owning" it*: When I question the value of who I am and what I bring to the table, I am no longer able to fit in naturally or make the contributions I'm truly capable of. There are always going to be people who try to marginalize you and what you contribute. I forgive their ignorance for not understanding what I'm saying and doing, and their built-in biases based on a host of misconceptions.

  At the end of the day, if I truly am giving it my all and doing what is needed, that's what matters. I tune out the critics and move on with what needs to be done. Accepting that not everyone is going to like or value me allows me to focus on the people who do.

◀◀

What's in Your Way?

You can never be too sure of yourself. There's an old saying, "The devil's in the details," and that saying applies definitely here.

You don't need to be a full-on self-saboteur to sabotage yourself. You can be firing on most cylinders and still be out a crucial one. What could have benefitted Paul and his team was to have a back-up plan in place—to anticipate things that could go wrong and prepare for them. They didn't anticipate for all that could go wrong; hopefully, they won't make that mistake again.

For most people, though, self-sabotage doesn't happen by missing a small detail. It's a culmination of missteps, miscalculations, and misperceptions. And the wrong behavior is a biggie.

Successful people make themselves stand out—and for the right reasons. They actively pursue opportunities in which they can stand out. This is a fairly known concept. As a communications coach, I have always been disturbed that so many people don't try to stand out. They avoid the spotlight and being set apart. They don't want to take chances and put themselves out there. Why? Fear is one reason. What if I take a risk and it backfires? What if I take a stand on something, and it pits me against my boss or even the CEO? What if my proposal changes the way that business gets done and eliminates jobs? What if my colleagues lose their jobs? What if I do, for speaking up?

The basic stance becomes that it is safer not to stand out, that it's better to follow the existing blueprint and not try to break the mold, or rock the boat, or any other beaten-to-death metaphor you can use.

Complacency can be far worse. Complacency is not the same as fear, but it can come from fear. Sometimes complacency happens because people are fearful to act; sometimes because they are comfortable and unmotivated. But it can have disastrous results.

Take for example the Madoff scandal. A recent *New York Times* article by Floyd Norris talked about the "confusion" at JP Morgan—about why no one ever reported any "suspicious activity." Says the author: "What the documents do show, however, is a huge bureaucracy where employees stuck to their own silos and did not communicate with others. Suspicions were there, but so were profits, and the profits seem to have outweighed any other concerns. Many people simply filled out and filed forms, oblivious to what those forms might, or might not, indicate."

Because no one questioned what was going on, millions of people lost millions of dollars. Lives were lost. Pensions evaporated. Had someone not been sleeping at the wheel, that person could have helped avert a huge crises and horrible suffering. That person could have been a hero. But the staff stuck to their "silos," and everyone came out looking bad.

Another element of this comes from the fact that we live in an "entitlement" mindset culture. We tend to think that things are supposed to happen for us, simply because they are. This is true for Boomers and Millennials and everyone in between—though each generation has its own reason.

Success is not about entitlement, though; it's about taking a calculated chance—not throwing a dart at a map and praying for clarity. It's about staying relevant and working to stay relevant. It's about being a person who matters; about rising above the ordinary.

Ordinary is a choice, but it doesn't come with success. Ordinary is a choice, but there are other options. It's time to break out of ordinary and become a success.

To self-sabotage is human. To transcend it...that's the tricky part, but that's the Holy Grail. That's success! First, though, you have to understand it.

▶▶

Words From the Wise—Julia Murney
Broadway Musical Theater Actor/Singer

Staying Relevant by Staying True

The big thing I have learned in my career as an actor is that there is no reason to be bullied into doing anything I don't want to do, even if it's the perfect choice for someone else. It's my life and my choice to make, whatever the outcome. I know why I make my choices, and in the end, that has to be enough for me (even if those around me may think I'm nuts). You need to keep your life relevant and hope that the career keeps following suit. Rebranding sometimes feels necessary when it seems as if everyone else is putting you into a box and deciding what you can and cannot do. I think you have to understand your strengths and decide when something's worth fighting for—to try and show that you may have something else up your sleeve.

◀◀◀

Understanding Sabotage

If someone ever asked me, "Karen, can you summarize how people sabotage themselves in one word?" I would have to give a resounding "No!" As we're seeing, sabotage isn't one thing people do to themselves, in spite of themselves. It would be much easier to address if it was that. But there are many words, and they usually work in groups.

Main Sabotage Makers

Fear	Procrastination
Impulsiveness	Narcissism
Avoidance	Ignorance
Stubbornness	Denial
Defensiveness	Narrow-Mindedness
Slovenliness	Unpreparedness
Arrogance	Desperation
Disorganization	Lack of imagination/ curiosity

This is a lot to cover, to be sure. The good thing is that we don't have to address every single one of these words to break free of them; self-sabotage can be snuffed out by having a basic awareness and thus correcting behaviors that lead to self-sabotage. In this chapter, we'll look at those behaviors. We'll identify common types of self-saboteurs, and look at how you may be sabotaging yourself.

Be sure to have your journal and working pen(s) handy! We spend a lot of time thinking about things and worrying about things, but a great way to get things under control is to write them down. Not only will having a concrete visual of the issues help you classify the issues, the act of writing itself helps build clarity.

Note: This needs to be an actual journal and an actual pen you're using—not typing, not an app, and not an audio file. It has been scientifically proven that handwriting on paper locks in an attitude or action better than typing or auto-recording.

Know Your Enemy

If you want to take down your enemy, you have to know your enemy. The better you understand your enemy, the more effective you can be. Self-sabotage is your enemy. The best way for you to combat it is to not only understand what it is, but why it is. You can't just press a button and it's done. You have to take it apart, piece by piece.

First, what's the "effect"?

What's going on (or not going on) in your life that isn't working? Are you not advancing at work? Is your relationship with your spouse or significant other unraveling? Are younger staff members not taking you seriously? Are older ones marginalizing you? What is it about your life that isn't working? Don't cop out and say "everything." I want you to really think about it.

Take out your journal and crack it open. On one page, list at least five things you feel aren't working out for you. If there are more than five, great; list as many as you need.

Look at your list. Are the things you listed separate or related? If your relationship isn't working, and your professional life is not working, does one fuel the other?

Now, what's the cause?

This is nowhere near as easy as the last challenge, but this is the root of all self-sabotage evil. This is where you need to have an "out-of-body" experience of sorts. It's time to try and do one of the hardest things there is to do; it's time to be objective about yourself.

We'll get into this more as we move through the book, but taking things personally is a major fueler of self-sabotage. And I know, you're thinking, "Karen, how can I think about me and have it not be about me—and have it not be personal?" Well, I'm telling you that not only can you think about yourself objectively, but you *must*.

So let's look at those areas you listed. Say the first one has to do with not having a great relationship with your boss. Write that down on its own on a single page, like this:

Marjorie hates me.

Now, under that, I want you to list the reasons why you believe this to be true, like this:

1. She yells at me in front of others.
2. She doesn't call on me in meetings.
3. She doesn't invite me to meetings.
4. She gave me a bad review.

And so forth.

Take your time with this. Don't stop writing to read—keep writing. If you start feeling depleted while you're writing all this out, take a break. Do something that makes you happy. Go to the gym. Watch a TV show you enjoy. Then get back to writing.

Once you've exhausted that list, save a page in between and start at the next reason. Repeat, saving a page between this and the next point.

Now that you have all of this written down, read what's there. Really read it, don't just skim through. What are you seeing? Do reasons repeat from one area to the next? Do your boss and your significant other yell at you in front of others—and for similar reasons? Circle issues that come up more than once. Use different color inks for different issues that repeat. Are you starting to see a pattern emerge?

▶▶▶

Why Not?—Kevin B. McGlynn
International Musical Theater Performer

"If you don't stop singing, I'm turning off the radio" is what I heard growing up, and as a result I grew up thinking I had no talent. So instead of working toward a career in performance, something I loved, I became a bank teller, something I didn't love. I had no idea what I was going to do with my life when someone overheard me singing on my break. She told me I had a great voice, which shocked me because of all the negative reinforcement I had growing up. I auditioned for the Boston Conservatory and was accepted.

I keep relevant in a competitive marketplace by showing up. I show up to auditions, to work on time, to opening nights, to industry parties, to benefits. I try to be where what's happening *is* happening, and make my presence known (in the literal and figurative sense). I keep my network active and growing, introducing myself to people I've never met, reconnecting with people from years past, keeping your degrees of separation minimal.

I stay informed. I believe you *must* keep yourself informed, know who and what is hot in your field, read related Websites, newspapers, and magazines. I also believe that you need to be able to have an intelligent conversation with a potential employer about the current state of things. It's not always talent or qualifications that get you the job; people want to know that you're an easy fit. No one wants to work with a diva.

I *love* the saying, "Success is when preparedness meets opportunity." I think it's important to know who you are as a performer or a professional, and to discover the roles and jobs for which you are appropriate and do your homework. I believe you should always know what you're getting into. When the incomparable Betty Davis was asked what advice she had for young actors coming up in the industry, she responded, "Learn your lines." It sounds sophomoric and simple, but I have learned that the better prepared you are, the more you can focus on your performance.

People in both the corporate world and the entertainment field have to grow thick skin to sustain negative feedback. A review is one person's opinion. Granted, that opinion may get printed for all the world to see, but it's still only one person's opinion. And opinions are like...well, you know, everybody's got one. Nobody's career is going to be made or broken by one good or bad review. If you're doing what you love, put your blinders on and continue to do it to the best of your ability.

◄◄

Types of Self-Saboteurs

The chances are that you do see "repeat offenders" in that list. Perhaps "hurts my feelings" or "makes me feel unmotivated" or "doesn't listen to me" are among them. The good news is that these "repeat offenders" will help you get to the root of the issues. Here are the main types of self-saboteurs:

► The Ostrich—If you ignore the problem or hide from the problem, the problem will go away. And you hide from it in plain sight.

► The Bear—If you bully the problem, wave your hands around, and growl menacingly at the problem, the problem will go away.

► The Skunk—You handle fear and rejection by getting defensive, by "shooting your stink" at others and making your shortcomings their problem.

► The Possum—You'd rather "play dead" than own your fears or mistakes.

► The Mole—You're not blind to the issues; you only see what you choose to see.

► The Lemming—You feel most comfortable just going along with the crowd, even if the crowd is swimming into a giant fisherman's net.

► The Salmon—You're constantly swimming upstream, against the current, to try and get to your goals.

► The Squirrel—You don't know where your "nuts" are.

► The Mosquito—You think the way to get results is to annoy them out of others by constantly buzzing around them.

► The Kangaroo—You jump from one thing to the next, never actually accomplishing anything.

► The Sloth—You're "never quite ready" to take advantage of any given opportunity that arises.

► The Pig—You think appearance is not everything, or perhaps "anything" to you—except it's mostly everything.

► The Peacock—The opposite of the Pig, you let vanity get in the way of opportunity.

► The Entitlement Beast (a.k.a. "Human")—You'll never see another "entitled animal" in the animal kingdom because an entitled animal is a dead animal.

You need to become aware. You need to be honest with yourself about how you're sabotaging yourself. You need to understand what self-sabotage is, and what about your behavior is self-sabotaging. It all starts with awareness. That you're reading this book is a great step in becoming aware!

▶▶

Words From the Wise—Cheryl A. Marshall, PsyD

Understanding Self-Sabotage

By definition, to sabotage means to deliberately destroy or obstruct for some advantage—military or political. But why would someone deliberately do this to oneself?

When it comes to self-sabotage, the problem with the definition is the word "deliberately." Self-sabotage is often an unconscious event, which makes the cure simpler than you'd think. The cure to self-sabotage lies in mindfulness, of self-awareness of your behavior, of taking responsibility and recognizing that with self-awareness of the behavior comes choice. Once you are aware of and in touch with your own behavior, you can make a conscious choice to stop sabotaging yourself.

There are countless ways to self-sabotage yourself, but here are the main ones I've seen affect people in my practice:

- ▶ *Procrastination:* Delaying or postponing meaningful action, which takes many forms, including arriving late. Few things shout out "I'm unreliable!" than recurrently arriving late.

- ▶ *Negative Thinking:* Many self-saboteurs focus on the wrong things in their lives. Instead of celebrating the positives, they are drawn like a moth to a flame to what is missing, what is lacking, what is wrong, which only attracts more negativity.

- ▶ *Comparing Yourself to Others:* When people compare themselves to others, they invariably end up feeling unmotivated. They feel like they will never be good enough because they aren't doing, getting, achieving in the same way as Joe or Susie, which results in poor self esteem and inertia.

- ▶ *Lack of Focus*: Many self-saboteurs feel adrift because they can't find meaning in their lives. Without purpose, what's the point?

► *Engaging in Bad Habits*: Some people smoke, over-sleep, don't exercise, or over drink. All of these are self-sabotaging behaviors that hold people back from achieving their goals.

Getting to the root of these will help begin to alleviate them. Remember, self-awareness is your most important and powerful tool for change.

◄◄

Reality Check

Look at the following questions and really think about them before answering. Your answers here will guide you in some of the ways you're allowing your life to sabotage you and help create guidelines to taking your life back.

► Do you have more than 10 things on your to-do list?

► When you have a big project ahead of you, do you look at the whole project or do you break it down into pieces?

► If you have a big task ahead, do you hide from it or roll up your sleeves to take it on?

► Do you opt out of things that are elective?

► When someone confronts you, do you listen? Do you withdraw? (Or is your safe place being the bully?)

► What's most important to you: past, present, or future?

► When something happens to you, do you react immediately or do you stew on it for a while?

► Do you willingly listen to advice?

► Do you have friends and mentors that are both older and younger than you? How do you choose them?

► Do you make "me time"? If so, how much?

► Do people come to you for advice?

► Are people open to working with you?

Let's break down the questions now.

1. Do you have more than 10 things on your to-do list?

If you answered yes, you are probably sabotaging yourself. On your to-do list, write down things that are out of the ordinary. "School pick up," "folding laundry," and "fixing dinner" are not what need to be on a to-do list. It's for out-of-the-ordinary things like "drop off camp forms" or "shop for Annie's birthday gift." People over-list and they are never able to cross everything off; that only creates frustration. Simplify.

2. When you have a big project ahead of you, do you look at the whole project or do you break it down into pieces?

If you answered "try to deal with it all at once," you are sabotaging yourself. The only way for you to properly absorb a big project is to break it down into its component parts and attack those parts one by one. Take baby steps. Otherwise, you're just going to overwhelm yourself, which will probably lead to procrastination and other bad things, most especially a project left undone.

3. If you have a big task ahead, do you hide from it or roll up your sleeves to take it on?

If you answered that you hide from it, in other words, put it off, you are sabotaging yourself. The phrase "You can do anything you put your mind to" is true, but it's oversimplified. Yes, you can overcome great obstacles and you can find the endurance to scale daunting, exhausting hurdles. But, as said previously, you have to break it down. Instead of hiding from something that has to get done, dissect it. Not only will you make the project seem more manageable, you'll also gain a greater sense of knowledge and intimacy with it—all winning things.

4. Do you opt out of things that are elective?

If you answered "yes," that you don't have to take an extra class or seminar or attend a meeting that could give you valuable information even though your presence is not mandatory, you are sabotaging yourself. If you're not ready or able to ask yourself "What do I have to gain from this," at least ask yourself, "What do I have to lose?" Going the extra mile always gets you ahead. Your progress may not be immediately trackable, but the more you gain, the more you can offer.

5. When someone confronts you, do you listen? Do you withdraw? (Or is your safe place being the bully?)

If you tend to withdraw from confrontation or lash out, you are sabotaging yourself. We're going to get into this much more deeply in Chapter 3, but you'd be surprised how many conflicts can be resolved quickly and painlessly if you just keep your cool.

6. What's most important to you: past, present, or future?

If you answered either "past" or "future," you are sabotaging yourself. You can't change the past; you can't control the future. You can keep your eye on the prize down the road, to keep you stimulated and engaged. But you have to stay focused in the present to be able to take one step at a time.

Where are you *right now*? Define it. Feel it. Understand it. Focus on the here and now.

7. When something happens to you, do you react immediately or do you think on it for a while?

If you react immediately, impulsively, in a kneejerk kind of way, you are probably sabotaging yourself, especially when a situation is charged with emotion. Things are often not as bad as they seem once the storm passes. React without thinking and you may find yourself burning some bridges.

8. Do you willingly listen to advice?

Simply listening to advice does not mean you have to take the advice, but opening yourself to other opinions and perceptions is important to finding a solution. If you just block out everyone's opinion except your own, you are sabotaging yourself. It's important to let the information come in, and for you to know how to filter it.

9. Do you have friends and mentors that are both older and younger than you? How do you choose them?

If you only listen to people who are older than you, you're missing out on a wealth of information about advances that have happened and have been studied about long after you've left the classroom. If you don't have mentors of all ages, you're probably sabotaging yourself.

10. Do you make "me time"? If so, how much?

If you don't have any time for yourself, you'll never know who you are, what you need to be happy, and what you need to get to achieve your dreams. If you make no time, or very little time, to be alone and think things through, you are sabotaging yourself.

11. Do people come to you for advice?

If no one asks your opinion about anything, it's a pretty good sign that people either think you're a hot mess, or that you're totally unapproachable. Of course both of these are sabotage! Being a hot mess is obviously so, but people feeling they can't approach you can trip you up in so many ways.

12. Are people open to working with you?

This goes along with the previous point. If people are not open to working with you, if they perceive you as being ineffective or bullying or unappealing or messy or disorganized or rude or...the list goes on... if no one wants to be on your team, you've got to figure out why, and you've got to change it!

▶▶

Words From the Wise—Cathy Russell
Actor/Teacher/Entrepreneur

Self-Sabotage

I have been involved so many times in my life with people who self-sabotage, but I never consciously self-sabotage. I work really hard not to. When someone gives me an opportunity, I go for it. I don't allow myself to sabotage myself.

When I see people engaging in self-sabotage—my students or my friends or my family—I say, "Stop it! Stop it right now!" When there is someone in our class who hasn't learned his or her lines and is reading off a phone, I call that person on it. "Why are you reading off your phone? Don't you know not to do it?! Learn the material. If you don't, you're going to say to yourself, the casting director didn't like me because I read off my phone." When I recognize self-sabotage in other people, I yell at them all the time.

◀◀

Who Can Help You?

Cathy Russell makes it a point to point out to her students when they are sabotaging themselves; whether or not they accept to hear it and act on what she tells them decides if they'll advance or not. People who are open to listening, people who can accept criticism with dignity and work to make strides to create shortcomings, these are the people who succeed. People who shut down from constructive criticism, who say "I'm sorry" all the time, who get defensive or are hurt, who crumble from hearing that what they are doing is not perfectly perfect, the "Ostriches," these people do not get ahead.

Don't get me wrong, I'm definitely not saying you need to listen to everything everyone ever tells you that you need to fix about yourself and follow that advice to a T. That would never work. What I'm telling you is that you need to construct a network of people you trust, who you know will be honest with you without being cruel, who want to see you succeed, and who have nothing personally to gain or lose whether you slump or soar. And you need to be willing to hear what they say and work on yourself accordingly.

I'll get into this more as we move through the book, but I have people like this who I call my "SPARC" buddies. It's a play on words—these people spark me to be a better me—but SPARC actually stands for:

Strategy

Purpose

Analysis

Rehearsal

Commitment

All of these are essential tools in fighting self-sabotage, and all can be facilitated with the help of a "buddy" because as this person helps you, you can also help this person.

Not having people in your life who you can honestly bounce things off of is a giant way people sabotage themselves. You know the phrase "No man (or woman) is an island." This is a big world full of opinions and perceptions. There's no way you can be objective about yourself and how you come across in the world. If you believe that you're the best judge of you, you're probably sabotaging yourself.

Not Staying the Course

Giving up is a huge way people sabotage themselves. They try to do something once, it doesn't work out, and they give up forever. I know so many people like this.

I know a woman whose biggest dream in life was to get her novel published. She worked on it for seven years. She handpicked seven agents she would send it to, agents she researched and believed would be the best candidates to represent her, the ones who would really get her and get behind her. When those seven agents rejected her, all for various reasons, from already having too full a client list to not connecting with her characters, she gave up. She put the novel in the drawer and never took it out again.

Loser.

I know a man who decided he wanted to go back to school and get the advanced degree in engineering he wasn't able to go after when he was younger because of the expense of having to take care of his young family. Finally when the kids were grown, he was able to take the bull by the horns and go back to school in order to get a better job. In his first semester, he got a D in physics. He quit school.

Loser.

Check out the "Why not?" stories you're going to find peppered throughout this book to find out what winners do.

▶▶▶

Words From the Wise—Gee Rittenhouse, PhD
Vice President and General Manager, Cloud and Virtualization for Cisco

Don't Celebrate Too Soon

My number-one job is to keep my people focused on the long-term objective and to keep them excited and engaged in the near-term objectives. But the most important piece is to actually keep the team challenged. When you have a brilliant long-term objective, people get very excited about it and they claim success at only 25 percent of the way, and then get off-track. "Look how far we've come! That's unbelievable! We're awesome now! This is super!" There's always this pressure within to relax.

We've accomplished something, so now let's relax. That's where complacency sets in. Celebrate the accomplishment, but it's important to keep them focused for the life of the goal, so they continue to follow through with the objectives.

◄◄

Bottom Line

Now that you know where you stand, and that there are ways to change your tendency to self-sabotage, it's time to take action. No matter how old you are, how set in your ways, you can still make a difference in your life.

2

Get Over Yourself

Your beliefs become your thoughts,
Your thoughts become your words,
Your words become your actions,
Your actions become your habits,
Your habits become your values,
Your values become your destiny.

—Oscar Wilde

Self-sabotage is universal but it's not terminal. It's fixable, but resolving it is a process. If you're willing to put in the work, you'll be able to reverse it and start living the life you want to live—a life that continues to fuel and energize you, not one that drains, exhausts, and demoralizes you. And you might have some fun along the way.

I've sabotaged myself in my career—we all have. But once I allowed myself to see the issues, I was able to tackle the issues. Once I was able to see myself, I was able to get over myself. I did it, and so can you.

It's all about baby steps—one day at a time. It starts with awareness of behaviors and acceptance, of owning those behaviors. When you can admit them and acknowledge them, you can change them. You can't change something you don't own.

▶▶

Words From the Wise—Rob Sedgwick
Film, Television Actor/Teacher/Author

What It's Really About

When I spot somebody shooting him- or herself in the foot, I advise that person to turn off their brain, because all your brain tells you is that you're fat, you're stupid and you're ugly and you're dumb and you can't do anything. It's really all it does. It's important to honor yourself, do the work, and be prepared.

One of our students paid a lot of money for a casting session. He canceled two appointments with me with less than 24-hours' notice. As a result, he wasn't prepared and I called him out for that. When he returned on another day, he was perfect and really grateful that I guided him.

I shared with him that when I was younger, when I was drinking and showed up to work late and unprepared, the guy who was in charge of the theater said to me, "I'll let it go this time, but remember, once is a mistake and twice is a bad habit. Don't ever do this again."

I know all about self-sabotage. I'm sober nearly 19 years, to which I credit a large extent to AA. AA saved my life. It gave me somewhere to go to talk and have support and have a program.

The thing is that you can put down the booze; it's just the beginning—it's dealing with all of the character flaws.

I'm grateful to be busy. Teaching enriches me. We love our students at Sedgwick-Russell. We have 90 students every six weeks and keep growing.

◀◀

Getting to the Root of Things

In the last chapter, we become aware of our internal sabotage triggers—of those aspects of ourselves that don't do us any good. However, the way sabotage manifests and the root of sabotage are different things. For Rob, the "booze" was only part of the problem. It's what brought the real problem to light—the obvious way he was hurting himself and his career. But the reason for the booze, the character flaws that prompted the boozing, was at the root of things.

Think of it like a medical condition. You can pinpoint and treat the symptoms (not getting ahead, not respected by colleagues, not heard in meetings, not hirable), but that doesn't make the "disease" go away. You can try to be less arrogant, less entitled, less timid, less fearful, but unless you tap these issues at the root, unless you understand and cure the "disease," you're not going to be able to sustain yourself.

To get over sabotaging yourself, you have to get over yourself, and you have to stop making excuses. For example, we live in a world full of "isms"—racism, sexism, ageism. For as much as anyone tries to fight these, they are a sad reality. You're just going to have to get over it. You're going to have to work around it. You can no longer use any "ism" of any kind as either a crutch or a shield. Be aware that they are there and strategize to roll with it. You can't reinvent out of it or away from it, but you can reinvent around it. You're going to have to roll with it.

This book is not designed to psychoanalyze you. That's a very specific and individual process. I'm a coach, not a psychiatrist, but I have coached psychiatrists to help them get over themselves and reinvent themselves.

Move Ahead by Letting Go

Know now that some people in your life will not support you. They may denigrate, ridicule, and even try to derail you. They may lie to you and tell you you're perfect just as you are. In this chapter, we're going to do an exercise to identify toxic people; and later, we'll get into how to get rid of them.

Whatever the case, just know that not everyone's going to be on board with your plan to reinvent and improve yourself. Some people will act out of jealously; others will act out of a sense of fear that, if you improve, you will become too good for them and they will lose you. Whatever the case, this can't hold you back. You have to keep moving forward with this reinvention. As Dr. Seuss has said, "Those who mind don't matter, and those who matter don't mind." Keep that as your mantra as you move forward.

Holding on to things is human, and sometimes it works to our benefit. Nurturing past professional relationships is a great example of this. Maybe you haven't worked for a company in five, 15, 30 years, but you maintain relationships you had in that situation. If those relationships are positive, energizing ones, that's a great thing and I encourage you to continue them. If they are not, it's time to let go.

Sometimes we hold on to people out of a sense of obligation. My client, Martha, had a situation like this going on with her, and her misguided sense of obligation and duty nearly ruined her career.

Martha began her career in public relations in the early 1990s, in the days when faxes were the exciting way to communicate electronically. Social media wasn't a term, but if it was, it had to do with members of the press who were friendly and outgoing.

As someone who had just graduated from college, Martha wasn't feeling particularly "social" herself. She was shy and terrified. She was so terrified, in fact, that she barely spoke to anyone. She always felt like the other assistants were whispering about her behind her back. She never felt comfortable around them, which was especially detrimental as she needed their help—they were the people she needed to ask if she had questions.

One day, while she was fumbling around at the Xerox machine, one of the longtime assistants, Jane, approached her and seemed to understand that Martha was struggling, without Martha telling her. Soon enough, Martha had learned from Jane all the ins and outs of the machine as well as all about the company. She also made a new friend. She kept in her mind and heart for a long time after, that if it hadn't been for Jane, she would have lost her job.

This loyalty almost cost Martha her career.

As time went on, Martha continued to prove herself at the company, enjoying small raises and special perks as a reward for putting in extra effort. Jane, on the other hand, seemed fine with the status quo. Wanting to keep Jane as a friend, Martha found herself turning down special projects at times, so as not to outshine Jane, which meant that other people the company were advancing and Martha was not.

Finally, she got her chance to become an executive, and she almost messed it up when Jane said to her, "I've been here longer than you! I should be the one being promoted!" Martha felt like she couldn't argue that with her, that had it not been for Jane, she'd be out on the street. She went to their boss and turned down the promotion, hoping that if she turned it down, Jane would get the job.

Not only did Jane not get the job, not only did it go to someone who had been at the company for merely a matter of months, but the "sheen" her bosses saw on Martha began to wear off. Where they'd once seen her as a person of high potential, with motivation and places to go, they now saw her as a "seat-filler," like Jane.

It wasn't until Martha left that company and stopped being so chummy with "dead weight" Jane that she started to advance in her career. Lesson learned.

Remember: Loyalty is a virtue. Loyalty to someone who might not deserve your loyalty can be a professional deathtrap. Just because someone helped you once doesn't mean you owe them forever.

Martha isn't the first person to be in that situation, and she won't be the last. As human beings, we do feel loyalty and obligation to others long past the "expiration date." Except the more we hold on the cement blocks that weigh us down, the more we sink when we should be swimming.

Dead Weight Detox Plan

This is something you'll be doing over the course of your life, but we're going to start here by looking at five prominent people in your life. Choose one from each of these areas:

1. Family.
2. Friends.
3. Professional life.
4. Hobby or avocation.
5. Community.

Open your journal and write each of their names at the top of a new page. Now, concentrating on each one individually:

- ▶ List five things that you like about that person.
- ▶ List five things that you don't like about that person.
- ▶ How do you feel before you see that person?
- ▶ How do you feel after seeing this person?
- ▶ Can you tell this person anything?

► How does this person enrich your life? Can you think of specific examples?

► Does this person detract from you? Again, use specific examples here.

It is incredibly important to be honest in this exercise. Consider this as simply an exploration for now. Just because your findings reveal your life would be a better place without this person does not mean you need to dump them today or even ever. My hope is that when you see, on paper, who in your life is "quality" and who isn't, you'll make it a point to give more of your time and yourself to the quality people, and sacrifice less of these things when you have to suffer the other. Toxic people just by association will sabotage you and aid you in self-sabotage. Don't engage in their energy.

Repeat this exercise at least once a week as you go through your contacts and associates and get a better idea of who you should hold on to and who you should seriously consider cutting loose.

But What if the "Dead Weight" Is You?

It's not just you that sabotages yourself by holding on to expired relationships. Sometimes, for unforeseen reasons not having anything to do with you, you become the expired relationship. That brings me to some very important points:

1. Not all relationships you need to let go are toxic.

2. Not all people you need to let go are the catalyst of your demise.

3. Sometimes the way others are around you is not the best for them.

4. If you are deemed "dead weight" by someone else, that's not always about you. (Sometimes it is, but much of the time, it isn't.)

What does this mean? Look at the case of Martha and Jane. Jane wasn't a bad person, nor was she particularly toxic. The issue in that relationship was that the women were operating at two completely different speeds.

Remember how I told you that ordinary is a choice? Just because someone doesn't want to get ahead doesn't make them a bad person. However, if you want to get ahead, a person like this is not a good match for you.

And you are not always a good match for others. It doesn't make you a bad or toxic person; it is what it is. The problem is that sometimes when our relationships end, not by our own doing, we personalize this. We obsess over it. When we do, we sabotage ourselves. Don't personalize it. Don't obsess over it.

Just because someone wants you out of their life doesn't mean it's about you. One of the best gifts you can give yourself is to move yourself out of the "center of the universe" and instead see yourself as an element within it.

Someone doesn't want to associate with you? Okay. Put your hurt feelings aside. Seeing everything as a slight to you is a sign of narcissism, and that's one of the big self-sabotage buzz words.

It's okay to grieve the loss of an associate or friend. It's okay to feel bad for a short time. But you have to put a timer on it. Set an actual timer. You may need to start at 30 minutes when the pain is fresh; maybe an hour. Set aside the time during the day and gradually lessen the time you're going to fixate on it. When the timer's up, so is your grief. At the sound of the bell, you're done.

Grieve, always grieve, and then move on. Wallowing in grief, wallowing in anything, is self-sabotage, and you have to stop it.

▶▶

Words From the Wise—Sharon Halley
Broadway Musical Theater Dancer/Choreographer

Take Advice!
During my long career, first as a dancer and then a choreographer, I've noticed there are patterns people have of shooting themselves in the foot and not getting anywhere. For example, there are people who don't go to every and any audition. There are performers who won't try to do what you ask them to do—they just say, "I can't" and that's the end of it. There are men who are too feminine when they dance, and women who are not at all feminine when they dance. I have seen all the above and they are deadly.

To help dancers break their cycle of sabotage, they have to take the first step. If they ask, "What did I do wrong," I will be as honest as I can about how they didn't hit the mark and what they might consider doing to improve. I never volunteer advice but I will give it when asked.

One of the ways I advise people to improve is to get as much experience as they can, to go to as many auditions as possible. Also, I encourage them to become aware of things outside themselves. I advise that the most important thing is to watch others around you, not with a critical eye but with an observant one. Take note of how other people react to various responses. You can learn a lot that way. Also, you must always try. No matter what is asked, just try it and really give it your all. If you don't understand what you're being asked, ask questions.

◀◀

Replace Rubbish With Role Models

As you continue to assess your circles and begin to see who deserves your love and your time, you'll be opening yourself to look for new people to click with—people who are going to fortify your life experience, not suck it dry.

Keep your eyes and your mind open to all people: younger or older, your sex or the other, your race or the other, gay, straight, and everything in between. The only parameters you should be putting on this exploration is that you're seeking people who inspire you; people who make you feel better about being you, about your life and your choices, and the choices you want to make; people who help keep you positive.

Now we're going to come back to SPARC:

Strategy.

Purpose.

Analysis.

Rehearsal.

Commitment.

You're going to be looking for people who can help you in your journey to become a more effective you; you're going to be looking to the people worth keeping in your life to get on board with you. You're going to be looking for people you can "bleed" with—that you can have a breakdown in front of, who can show you compassion, for people you can really trust.

A SPARC buddy should be someone who's not in any kind of competition with you. It should be someone close to you, perhaps a cousin, friend, former colleague, or an in-law. Siblings, spouses/partners, and parents are generally not the best SPARC buddies because the relationships can sometimes be too close to be properly objective, but everyone's different. It should be a person you're comfortable enough to speak frankly with, a person you can say "enough" to when you're feeling too overwhelmed by their advice.

SPARC™ Worksheet

A SPARC buddy helps you with *strategy*. By listening, weighing things, and asking open-ended questions (see Chapter 7 to learn how), this person can help you formulate your reinvention plan.

A SPARC buddy helps you with *purpose*. Do you know where you're going to? Probably not, which is why you've landed in this pit of self-sabotage. A SPARC buddy can help you figure out what it's all about by asking the tough questions and encouraging you to be honest with the answers.

A SPARC buddy helps you with *analysis*. This is not like Freudian analysis. Your SPARC buddy is not your shrink. Rather, he or she helps you analyze your options and figure out which are the most positive for you.

A SPARC buddy helps you with *rehearsal*—meaning that this is a person who will not only help you plan your journey, but also practice with you as you get more confident in finding your way.

A SPARC buddy helps you connect with your reinvention plan and then helps you *commit* to it. You need to lose weight? She or he reminds you why, and keeps you on track, gently reminding you of your intent when you unintentionally have another piece of cake.

A SPARC buddy should be someone with whom you share core principles, and someone who is also able to put aside his or her stuff to help you figure out yours. It's a person who can help you find that missing part of you. A SPARC buddy holds the map while you drive.

In an ideal world, a SPARC relationship is a reciprocal one, but sometimes it doesn't work out that way. It's okay as long as there's an openness and understanding about things. No one wants to feel like they're being taken advantage of.

SPARC-ing the Conversation

Sometimes getting started is the hardest part, so following are some open-ended questions you can provide for your SPARC buddy to ask you. (Note: Open-ended questions using who, what, where, when, why, and how will elicit a more fully formed response, not just a "yes" or "no"):

ASK: What are you trying to accomplish?

NOT: Is this what you're trying to accomplish?

ASK: What did you discover about that online course?

NOT: Did you enjoy the online course?

ASK: How are you going to communicate your plan?

NOT: When are you going to communicate your plan?

ASK: What is your time frame?

NOT: Do you have a deadline?

ASK: Where do you want to be this time next year?

NOT: Do you want to be with X Company next year?

ASK: Who will be on your list for skills development?

NOT: Is Jane on your list?

As for *you* asking your SPARC buddy for help, be as specific as possible about what you need. Remember, your buddy is providing a free service because she or he is your ally. Respect that this is a favor to you.

Examples:

- ► I need guidance in communicating my unhappiness to some-one who continually makes me:
  - ▷ Feel bad about myself.
  - ▷ Tries to compete with everything I say and tries to one up me.
  - ▷ Is unavailable to me emotionally.
- ► Who do you think I should speak to in addition to a therapist about my struggle?
- ► What books, lectures, online tutorials do you know of that could help me?

We'll get more into the nuances of clear communication later in Chapter 7, but this is a good start in knowing how to effectively communicate with others.

▶▶▶

Words From the Wise—Deborah McCarthy
Director, Results Delivery Organization, Alcatel-Lucent

I Open Myself to Others

My mentors' long-term commitment and support has helped me grow and kept me anchored in reality. They're my cheerleaders and toughest coaches when they need to be. I've been very fortunate and have built a network through time that influenced and shaped my views and choices. The truth from a trusted source, who has only my best interest in mind, is a rare gift. And to each of them, I've tried to be their cheerleader and coach in return.

During my toughest struggles, they are always there for me, providing encouragement and support. And when I'm about to walk off a cliff, which I have done a few times, they're there to warn me or patch me up after I go over. Just like in marriage, they're there in good times, bad times, and sometimes just-to-have-fun times.

◀◀◀

SPARC Buddy Search

Once you've made some progress in listing those people who energize you and those who drain you, you might start seeing potential SPARC buddies in the group of people that enrich your life.

A SPARC buddy should be:

▶ Positive.

▶ Open-minded.

▶ Resourceful.

▶ A good listener.

▶ Non-judgmental.

▶ Objective.

▶ Compassionate.

▶ Fun.

▶ Someone you enjoy being around.

Is there anyone you know that can be described by most or even all of these words? Keep referring back to your journal as you decide who's worthy to be your SPARC buddy—and also to whom you might be a good buddy.

It's Not Just About the People

Several years ago, I decided to sell my home, a fairly spacious house, and move to an apartment that was a fraction (a small fraction) of the living space I had grown accustomed to for over 20 years. The move was important for me. I wanted to be closer to the theater scene that makes up half my career. I knew the proximity and the energy of Manhattan was going to be great for me. It was going to be a real boost to that part of my life.

The issue was, though, how was I going to fit all of my stuff into a smaller space like that? Of course I wasn't going to be able to bring it all with me, and that was also the point. Some of those years in that house had been wonderful; some had been tragic. It was time for me to part with the past, and a great way for me, for anyone, to do this is to part with "stuff."

What's good about stuff is that it's tangible. Though it may not be easy to part with the hurt you feel over a divorce or other loss or rejection because you can't hold that pain in your hand, you can hold stuff in your hand, and hand it off to someone else.

Armed with Tim Gunn's *A Guide to Quality, Taste and Style*, I went through my belongings and gave away or sold more than 90 percent of what I had. It was painful; it was grievous. But after the dust settled, and settling on much less that needed to be dusted, it was freeing.

However, whether it's people, stuff, or behavior, so many of us walk around dragging so much dead weight behind us. As we're fixating on keeping all of this unnecessary stuff in balance, we're missing out on opportunities to collect and carry better stuff—better opportunities, better relationships, better living through letting go.

▶▶

Words From the Wise—James Gerth
Communications Coach/Theater Director

Get Out of Your Way
We have many excuses for failure. "I stepped on my own toes." "I tripped over myself." "I was my own worst enemy." "I psyched myself out." "I got in my own way." Most of the time, these negative feelings are a self-fulfilling prophecy. I have seen it countless times in both my careers, as an actor and as a communications skills consultant. I have, of course, experienced it in myself in both fields. I have learned from my mistakes.

For a majority of actors, the most stressful part of the business is the audition. Standing in front of strangers, you are asked to display every possible talent you possess, shape those talents to fit a particular job, and do that better than the other 400 actors standing outside the door listening to you, waiting to do better than you. If that were not enough, you have no more than three minutes or as little as 30 seconds to do it.

Since I became an actor four decades ago, hundreds of thousands of actors have walked out of auditions and said to themselves, "I don't get it; I hit that note in the shower a hundred times. Why couldn't I do it in there?" Or, "I was worried about getting the lyrics wrong and I was right. I got them wrong. Why did I blow it?"

The answer is very simple: you talked yourself out of it. The human brain is a powerful thing. You can use it for great success or great failure. You just need to be committed to which you want. As much as you want to succeed, if you don't focus on that success as the eventual outcome, you leave room for doubt. That doubt is what you trip over with your own two feet. The audition is not unlike a sales call or job interview, where your audience will pretty much make up his or her mind in about 30 seconds if they should consider you seriously.

On the communications skills side of things, some clients I have trained will say: "When I speak in front of groups, I know I'll get nervous. So I start with a joke because it calms me down." Other self-imposed roadblocks include "I know he doesn't like me; it will be a tough sell," or "I always have a hard time getting through to them," or "I never know the right thing to say."

The psychological evaluation would be that you know you are going to fail, so you make your excuse ahead of time as to why. Once you have committed yourself to failure, you are bound to succeed at that failure. Now imagine what happens if you spend the same energy and focus on the commitment to success?

There are always plenty of hurdles to success. Why create even more? It is far better to use these hurdles as an opportunity to improve or as a jumping-off point for you to present yourself and your product or service as a way for your customer to remove these hurdles.

Every encounter in business—show business and corporate business—is an opportunity. I have an opportunity to show off my talent. I have an opportunity to share good information with you from which you can profit. If we turn these opportunities into challenges, we create obstacles.

If you stop focusing on all the reasons why you will succeed at failure, your brain will have room for you to focus on your audience and your customer. You will be able to listen to their needs and follow their direction. You will be able to bring the best of you to the task at hand. Get out of your way and let yourself succeed.

◀◀

The Great Inhibitor

In all my years, and there have been a lot of them, I've seen people ruin their lives and careers more with fear than anything else. We're always told that nothing is ever as bad as we fear it will be, and yet, we still allow fear to flatten us. Why do we give so much power to fear? Why do we expend so much energy on "I can't" instead of on "I can"?

What if we lived without fear? What if we took chances on things? What if we let ourselves grow by going out and grabbing all the opportunities we could, by forcing ourselves to experience things, by allowing ourselves the chance to fall, to give ourselves the chance to get up again?

One of the main fuels of fear is the idea of rejection. No one likes rejection. Employees and performers alike tie their stomachs in knots over a bad review. What if you could separate yourself from your reviews? What if you could compartmentalize better? What if you could draw a line between yourself and what others thought of you? You'd probably fear less and live more. We'll get more into this in later chapters.

▶▶▶

"Why Not?"—Robert Diamond
CEO, BroadwayWorld.com

I come from a tech background so I've always been a geek at heart. I started on computers at a very young age. I got into programming and all of that, and when I was a senior in high school, I was building little Websites on the side. I cofounded a computer club at my high school, and because I had early dismissal, I was able to take a job as a junior Webmaster for a local media company.

Around the same time, my parents had taken me to see *The Phantom of the Opera*. It was the Broadway show that flipped the switch for me. I became a big fan of Michael Crawford after listening to his recordings and went to see him at a Vegas show that he was doing at the time.

In college at Syracuse, I started my own Website, Diamond Online, which had a page for the Yankees, a page for the school, and a Michael Crawford page. That Michael Crawford page was the second-biggest Michael Crawford fan page on the Internet. But "second biggest" didn't work for me. I was always trying to think of ways to improve it and make it the biggest. Then one day, a woman wrote to me complimenting my page, and offering me stuff to scan. I accepted, and two weeks later, 24 boxes arrived at my dorm.

When I launched this giant Michael Crawford Website three or four months later, I got a legal letter from Michael and his charitable fan association saying that I violated six or seven thousand copyright laws, and not only was I going to go to jail for that, but I had also posted pictures online that they were selling for charity. I wrote back, saying, "Instead of suing me, why don't you hire me for no money to make an official Website for you guys and Michael Crawford?" Thankfully, they said yes.

I started doing that as a freshman and kept at it, also working for the same publishing company I had in high school. When I graduated in 2001, they hired me full time. At that point, the company had grown from about six people to about

60 people, so I was managing a whole department of Web developers and Web designers, but still always in the background, I was in love with the theater world.

In 2002, Michael came back to Broadway in *Dance of the Vampires*. I made his whole Website, and in the process, started looking at the theater Websites. That's when the idea for BroadwayWorld started germinating in the back of my brain. I launched it in 2003.

The Website has grown, every day, month, year, and quarter since its inception. Every day we're doing something new and trying to expand in a different way, taking a look at what we did yesterday, and seeing how it can be done better today and tomorrow.

◄◄◄

Anything You Can Do, I Can (Can't?!) Do Better

One of the biggest ways you can sabotage yourself is to compare yourself to anyone else. The race you're competing in needs to be against yourself. When you start thinking things like "Fred's boss gives him a quarterly bonus; why doesn't mine?" or "Linda made partner after two years at the firm, but I've been here three!" you're setting yourself up to fail.

Remember, again, the line you need to draw between your thoughts and feelings, and how you come across in the world. Remember Jane, who complained to Martha about not getting ahead, and neither woman won. You need to focus on you, what you can offer, what you can deliver, and what you deserve—not based on the merits and/or rewards of anyone else.

▶▶

Words From the Wise—Cheryl A. Marshall, PsyD

Refocusing on You

Don't focus on others; focus on yourself. Write down the five accomplishments of which you are most proud. Write down the five qualities that you most love about yourself. If you can't think of any, ask a friend to help you. A great way to stay focused on the "goods" you have to offer is to wear a tangible reminder of your successes and value. Maybe a watch or a ring—something you can wear daily. When you look at it, you will think about you and all you've accomplished. Remember: It's all about you.

◀◀

The Forest for the Trees Exercise

Do you know what this phrase means, "Can't see the forest for the trees"? It means you're so caught up on the little things, you can't see the big picture. When you're caught up on little things, it means you're not focusing, and if you're not focusing, you will not be succeeding.

What are the "trees" in your life that getting in your way? Are you able to stand back and look at the trees? Take out your journal. At the top of the next available page, I want you to list every single thing that's pressing on you today; every one, not just work-related things. If you have a family, be sure to list things like "make the school drop off" or "make breakfast/lunches" and "homework help" along with things like "e-mail the team about the big project"—every single detail, every single tree.

When you're done, pull away from your list and see what's there. Dr. Marshall says, "Many self-saboteurs feel adrift because they can't find meaning in their lives. Without purpose, what's the point." I say, before you can find purpose, you need to see what you're up against. You need to categorize, organize, and prioritize. Not everything is going to get done today.

Find what matters, what really matters, and start planning your "forest" that way. Your forest is your purpose—cultivating it, nurturing it, letting it grow. Which of these things are your strong, mighty oaks? Which of them are your overgrown weeds?

And Then What?

People can get to the top of the crop, slaying all self-sabotage dragons in their way. And yet, once they've achieved their goal, this is the point where many implode into self-sabotage. Why?

When you've hit the mark, how do you then go and top yourself? There was a reporter who lived his whole life with one goal in mind: Winning the Pulitzer Prize. He did, and then he committed suicide shortly thereafter.

You need to have a goal after the goal, a "When, Then."

In addition to having more goals beyond the goal, you need to be flexible about the goals. Your goal cannot define you, as much as you can't let your life define you. Nothing outside your control can define you. A divorce, a death of a loved one doesn't define you. There can't be one single event that defines you.

When Jane Fonda turned 70, she had this feeling that she had gotten to the top of her "mountain." What was there left for her to do? She decided: Find the next mountain," and that's what she did and continues to do. And that's what successful people continue to do.

What's next? How long can you dance? Explore new things. Have more than one goal. Whatever you do, just keep those goals grounded in reality. If you're 70, you're probably not going to start learning ballet on pointe at this point in your life. However, some ballroom dancing?

Here are the top five things you *do not* do when you attain your goal:

1. Do not become complacent.
2. Do not shut down.
3. Do not give up.
4. Do not think you have no more purpose.
5. Do not wait to die.

Here are the top five things *you do* when you attain your goal:

1. Do look forward to each day.
2. Do continue to see life as an adventure.
3. Do seek out the "fresh wonder" in life.
4. Do set the new goal, and begin to plan your strategy to achieve it.
5. Do have more than one thing you can look forward to.

▶▶

"Why Not?"—Karen Arlington
Actor/Singer

In 2009, I was asked to join a singing group. I hadn't sung professionally for a few years, and I thought, "Hey, sounds like fun!" It also didn't hurt that we were going to get great exposure in and around the New York metropolitan area. What I did not know was that in order to be part of this group, I had to learn formation choreography (stage movement done with surgical precision, a la Radio City Music Hall's Rockettes).

I had never had a dance lesson in my life except for a few months of ballroom dancing as a kid growing up in Denver. That did not prepare me for the mental—and dare I say, physical—anguish I endured given the demands of this performance group. It was humiliating, exhausting, frustrating, and maddening. The progress I made was infinitesimal, and all the while, we were performing live in front of hundreds of people several times a year at Lincoln Center.

So many times, I wanted to bolt. So many times, I cried myself to sleep, blaming heredity, my being deaf in one ear (why that would have anything to do with dancing, I haven't a clue), the choreographers, the director, anything, anyone, rather than gripping the problem by the neck and wrestling it to the ground.

And, how often did I hear my friends and family say, "Karen, you are feeling so miserable; please quit the group. And by the way, you're not very good at formation choreography."

Not very good? I was terrible.

When you are on stage with people, some professional dancers, and others who have had ballet lessons as a child or have been in musical theater performing formation choreography, they know the terminology. They know what it means when a choreographer at the first rehearsal says, "Now eight counts on box step into eight counts grapevine into eight counts chasse."

I felt as though I had just landed on Mars. And it wasn't just the feet I had to worry about. Arms have to be at a specific angle above your head, and hands have to be in a specific shape, with a specific finger elevated at a specific height. I could give them a finger all right, just not the one they wanted.

It was torture.

My colleagues on stage thought they were being helpful by saying, "Karen, you're musical; just feel the music." "Karen, stop thinking and just *do*."

Do? DO WHAT?

One person in the early days of the group even lobbied the other performers and the director to get me off the stage entirely during group numbers. Oh, and did I mention that all the time we were singing and acting while dancing? Sing and act I can do, but all three at the same time? Not so easy.

My Irish temper finally got the better of me. As much as I wanted to run away, quitting would have meant defeat and I don't do defeat.

I made a plan. I stuck to that plan. I struggled. I fought. I worked. I gave everything I had to making it work. I lost sleep. I lost friends. But finally, I got it. Now, after five years and many, many frustrations and failures, after scores of live performances, I'm less terrible. I'll never be amazing, but I can hold my own. And the really good news is that now when I'm booked in a theatrical production that involves intricate stage movement, I know the terminology, and I can count on my team of advisors and coaches to help me.

I didn't "dream." I didn't quit. I "acted"—and that made all the difference. I learned a really important lesson in the process. If you are so ignorant about a subject that you can't even formulate the questions to ask about what you're learning, you'll be stuck. You have to find people who can coach you below basic level. Those people aren't always the best performers, but they can be masterful at teaching. I learned the most about dance technique from my voice teacher, who is not a trained dancer, but he certainly understands rhythm and knows what it takes to break down the components of stage movement. Even better, he knows how to teach the components step by step until the choreography is locked in your brain. It was an amazing take away from the experience.

So, sure I know what it is to struggle. But I also know what it is to succeed. You can't have one without the other, but you can succeed. Anyone who tries can succeed.

◄◄◄

Bottom Line

Yes, Karen Arlington is my stage name. Did you guess? When I told you I have been through this process before, I wasn't kidding. I have been through it before and I will go through it again because there's always room to grow—until we die. And we are all going to die someday. That's why you have to make your life and the time you're given really count!

Preventing the scythe of self-sabotage from slashing your success is a lifelong, endless process. As we move through this book, we'll find ways to keep growing as successes as we grow away from being saboteurs—self- and otherwise.

PART 2

REVIEW! RENEW! REINVENT!

One of the reasons people end up trapped in a perpetual "hamster wheel" is that they've come to believe that they are too far along in whatever career they're in to switch gears. They're used to what they do, what they've always done, and they don't think they can reinvent. They've been spinning in that wheel for so long that they've lost sight of the fact that it isn't going anywhere.

How old is too old to reinvent yourself, to discover your true passion and work toward it? How old is too old?

The catch-all buzz-term we like to throw around, "society," dictates that older is not better, that to become older is to become increasingly irrelevant. Ordinary people buy into ideas like that and keep busying themselves in the assembly line of their career. They keep spinning in the hamster wheel.

The fact is that you're never too young or too old to reinvent yourself. No matter what age you are, when your professional or personal life isn't working, it's time to reinvent it—to reinvent yourself.

Successful people sniff out the trends, stay ahead of the next wave of opportunities, keep learning, and are curious about everything. Successful people don't let ideas like that one dictate their actions and undermine what they can achieve.

Said Billy Crystal in a recent *New York Times* interview, "When you get to a certain age, [producers, film company executives]...hesitate a bit.... They're not sure there's an audience. I said 'There's 77 million [seniors] in this country wanting a story for them.'"

Jerry Seinfeld, now pushing 60, started a new series online, *Comedians in Cars Getting Coffee*. Performer Andrea Martin is 67 years old and played a physically demanding role in Broadway's *Pippin* night after night. She said in an *Entertainment Weekly* article: "The truth is, I'm really scared of heights... But when I'm up there, I'm not frightened. I feel younger and very vital as a woman. And why shouldn't I?"

Successful people don't take "no" for an answer.

No hesitation. No defeatist thinking. The fear is there, but it's faced night after night. That, combined with taking responsibility—for yourself and your life—is what makes reinvention and success possible. Do the work, do it in a focused manner, and you'll get the results you seek.

In the last section we talked about self-sabotage; in this section, we'll look at how to "re-invent" yourself out of it. Think of reinvention as a kind of antidote to self-sabotage. Self-sabotage is cutting yourself at the knees, making yourself a worse person, whereas reinvention is nurturing your passion, intellect, and other qualities to become the best person you can be.

This section is your toolkit. Here, you will find the tools you need to stop sabotaging your dreams and your actions, and also those it takes to help you grow.

I'll show you how to readjust your attitude. Without a positive attitude, you're going nowhere. Without positive people surrounding you, you'll be stuck in the fail zone. I'll give you tips and tricks to improve yours and get you into the right mindset for achieving your goals.

I'll train you to re-train your focus. Without a carefully mapped out strategy, you're going to be driving in circles, no matter how much ambition you have. (Ambition is like a car with a full tank of gas; focus is like your GPS.) I'll help you figure out what your strategy is and how to map it out, including how to find a "buddy" to help you through.

I'll help you with looking your best. Impressions of us are formed the minute we walk into a room. It's difficult to break one's first impression of you, so you better make sure it's the very best you that people see when entering a room. Yes, you can judge a book by its cover, and you always do. The same goes for other people. I'll show you how to look your best—how to be the book others can't help but be compelled to pull off the shelf.

I'll help you come across in the best possible light. Though appearance is how you look, "image" is an extension of you beyond that—it's about your personal brand and how you're coming across in the world. I'll help you figure out what that is and learn to spread it successfully.

I'll help you communicate. Do you speak effectively? How well do you come across in a world where most of what people know of you is tapped out in quick keystrokes, in 140-character tweets, and in YouTube videos that are 60 seconds or less? I'll help you maximize your voice in this low-attention-span world.

I'll guide you in growing your aptitude. You can only "fake it 'til you make it" to a point. Without solid education and training, you're dead in the water. I'll teach you how to get off your butt and seek opportunities for enhancement and enrichment.

I'll coach you in fueling your ambition. There's a difference between being driven and driving. There's a difference between being pulled and pushing toward your goals. What's the secret to being ambitious and staying that way? I'll show you here.

And I'll show you how to keep believing in you—even when the results don't always seem obvious. How can you get over yourself without believing in yourself? I'll also give you tricks and tips to feed your soul. To inspire confidence and keep nurturing it as you work to achieve your goals.

Committing yourself to navigating away from self-sabotaging actions and behaviors will get you on the road to reinventing yourself into the person you were always meant to become—but never before allowed yourself to become.

3

Attitude

If you want to make God laugh, tell him about your plans.
—Woody Allen

Life isn't always what you plan on. You can create a blueprint for how you think or how you would like for things to go in your life, but you can't expect that the universe is going to follow that plan.

To become successful, of course, you must have some plans. There has to be a strategy in place. It's not like you'd ever take a road trip without using a map of some kind. (Wait, you would? Then Chapter 4 is one chapter you need to pay special attention to!) But not everything you're going to encounter can be found on your map. A fresh detour, a jackknifed tractor-trailer that causes a backup that adds hours to your journey—on your road trip, these are things you need to take in your stride.

Your life is the same way.

So you planned on becoming a partner in the law firm you've spent the past 10 years working nights and weekends at to get ahead. So you decided that when you got out of college you would work your way up the ranks and become editor-in-chief in the publishing firm where you got your first job. So you wanted to shine on Broadway, and you spent the better part of your childhood in lessons and rehearsals and at auditions while your friends partied and hung out.

And maybe your ankle gave out and you weren't able to dance again. And maybe the economy went belly-up and most of the publishing industry, you included, was downsized out of jobs. And maybe the newly appointed managing partner of your firm remembers (or mis-remembers) having a serious rivalry with you in law school and now holds something of a vendetta against you.

Not all sabotage is your fault, and maybe life does try and sabotage you sometimes. Okay, much of the time. But here's the thing: it's not that life trips you up with its many and varied complications that matters; it's how you handle these complications that matters.

So Now What?

It's like that old saying, "When life gives you lemons, make lemonade!" I'm a big maker of lemonade; I've made a ton of it with the bushels of lemons life's thrown at me. How about you?

Let's say you just lost your job. You got laid off, and yes, it was probably unfair, unjust, and possibly cruel. In many large companies, when someone, let's say the word, gets "fired," security and HR usher that person to the door as they carry away a small box of personal belongings. They take away your laptop and your phone. The experience is humiliating and unsettling. The ground beneath you seems gone. Maybe you worked for that company for years and had always been a trusted employee. Now you're being treated like a criminal, probably for no act of malfeasance, but just being the "box" on the flowchart, management decided they could do without you.

Your life has now changed, forever. We all know that when we dictate the life change, though it's still stressful, we're in control. But when someone else dictates your life change, it's traumatic.

This firing, this "letting you go," will not be what defines you, though. Although many people deny their anger, or feed their anger for months, even years, it's something that needs to be dealt with in stages so it doesn't swallow you. So you can become the *you* who happened to have this experience, not the you who let it cripple you for good.

While "Stay Positive" makes for a great bumper sticker, it's not human or possible to jump right into the idea of seeing the roses for the thorns. It's not reality. Sometimes you can't. Sometimes you have to feel sorry for yourself for a little while. You have to grieve for a few moments. Just notice that I said "moments" here, not decades.

Remember in Chapter 2 where we talked about grieving over the loss of a friend or associate who no longer wants you in his or her life? That's exactly how you're going to handle this now. Set an alarm clock for 30 minutes a day for a week; then 15 minutes a day for a week; then five minutes a day for a week. And then stop. See how you're doing and see if you can stop the grieving. You need to isolate the grieving moments because grieving can become addictive, and that's only going to sabotage your future endeavors!

Here's a plan I give to my clients. I have attributed a timeline to it (a week, a month, etc.) but that's when I'm able to assess the situation individually. For the purposes of this book, I will break the process in steps instead.

Importantly, at each of these steps, I want you to get yourself a little treat. I'm not saying to spend money you don't have, but a small indulgence like an ice cream cone or downloading songs or getting a manicure can go a long way.

Step 1: Damage Control

As angry as you are, as crazed and broken as you feel, do not, *do not* start posting away on Facebook about how angry you are. You have to tell close family members and close friends right away, but you don't have to tell anyone else. Before sharing the news, spend some time on your own. *Find your calm.*

People are going to be hurt and confused over this news, and it may seem to you that they are angry *at* you. Chances are that they are not; they're angry *for* you. You need to get yourself in a place of calm where you'll be strong enough to see the difference.

Step 2: Post Mortem

Yep, this is just what it sounds like. Once you've gotten over the initial shock and you've had a little distance from the situation, it's time to break it down. This is a good time to bring in that SPARC buddy. Was the situation unavoidable? Was there something you could have done, or shouldn't have done, that may have changed what occurred? If you can't do this without anger, it's best to wait a few more days and give yourself a little more distance before the dissection.

Step 3: Strategy

What are you going to do now? The last thing I ever advise anyone to do in this situation is to start looking for a job right away. Do you really want to be the boozy sad-sack in the bar so desperate for comfort that, to fill this new void, you're ready to go home with anyone? No way! Your new endeavor is way too important. Instead of throwing your sorry self at potential employers, spend time on yourself. Meditate, exercise, and clear your head. Take a class in something that interests you. Rediscover who you are. You may find that going back into the same kind of job you came from is not what you want out of life after all. But you will never know that until you explore.

Step 4: Do

Now that you've had a break and you can start to see more clearly, you're going to have a much stronger self to put out there for your next adventure. Now is the time to get out there and conquer the world.

What It Comes Down To

People who sabotage themselves don't see things this way. People who sabotage themselves retreat into the corner, curl up in a ball, and blame. "If it wasn't for Jack, I'd have gotten that promotion!" "If it wasn't for the greedy banking industry swallowing financial security from my company, I'd still have a job!" "If it wasn't for that choreographer demanding I follow that complicated routine with all that footwork, I'd still have a chance to dance!"

People who sabotage themselves are snarling, bitter, and angry. They see setbacks as being just that and nothing more. I'm a big believer in failure. You can't be a success until you fail and feel good about failing. Of course you can have regrets, but regret can't be something that defines you.

People who succeed see setbacks as opportunities. They realize that though they may have "set a course" for themselves, due to matters completely out of their control, that course has been changed. They know this means it's not time to pull over to the side of the road, roll up all the windows, and die. They know this means it's time to chart another course.

Are you a soggy, saggy bag of unhappiness? Or, even worse, are you a seething cauldron of anger and resentment? (Did you know that anger increases your risk of heart attack by about 5 percent and stroke by about 3 percent? We're all going to die, but do you really want your death to be because of your own anger?)

Well, do something about it. No one wants to hang out with a sad sack. In this chapter, I'll share with you what I know about the power of positive thinking. Yes, it's a real thing. I'll show you how maintaining a positive outlook will help keep you grounded. Because it's not just me who knows this; all successful people know this.

▶▶▶

Words From the Wise—Melissa Errico
Broadway Musical Theater Actor/Singer

Overcoming Adversity

When I was in the hit New York revival of *Passion*, I had bronchitis but continued with every performance. The cough and congestion was not interfering with my voice, until one night I felt weak. I had to step out of the show and let the bronchitis run its course. An ordinary bad cold to some, but a nightmare for a soprano! Due to complications with the infection or the act of coughing, I developed a small injury which my doctor decided would best be eradicated by laser surgery. That was my best bet to return to a clean bill of health. I had to remain silent for three months—no singing and no talking, which wasn't easy to do with small children.

The challenges were many—psychological and professional. I had to step out of the show. I had to face that I had become bad for business and they terminated my contract. Though I understood the business aspect, I was devastated and heartbroken. It is one of the hard lessons of life to separate the personal from the business aspects. I had to learn more about separating myself from events around me. I had to deepen in self-respect and learn to be patient with my body.

I did many things to heal myself after the vocal cords were deemed healed and well. I tried many Reiki sessions (essentially a gentle meditative practice with a master who works with "universal energy") and returned to occasional yoga. I settled on regular acupuncture (the Five Points method), a good low carb/low sugar/no caffeine diet, and some running. I believe the act of sweating is *very* therapeutic. I began to see a cognitive behavioral therapist, who helped me to think through how I react to things. I consciously work to be less negative, to seek immediate solutions to today's tasks and not get swept into long lists of worries. Also, I am finding the lighter side of situations, looking for chances to laugh and have pleasure. (It's not a crime to find comfort and enjoy a pastime!) Being less hard on others and on myself can be very uplifting. In relation to a crisis, I now recognize that very few people are actually paying sustained attention to *you* and have a thousand reasons for their actions. Try not to take things so personally! "Move on," as Stephen Sondheim said in his famous song of that title from the Broadway musical *Sunday in the Park with George*.

When there's been a trauma in your life, you can emerge stronger. Like any mythic journey, you endure things (Slay the dragon! Overcome great hurdles!) and can really deepen yourself—your spirit, your consciousness—in the end.

I chose not to become scared and resentful and disappointed. I didn't know I was doing that. I just kept moving forward and doing things that seemed good for me. I hadn't moved much in those three silent months, so slowly I walked and then swam and did exercise to try to return to the normal world. I returned to singing and took baby steps each day to return to my career and to find work. A year later, I have a new musical on my plate!

I have heard people say you can grow stronger from being brought to the very bottom. I don't want to sound dramatic, but I do think I never could have imagined feeling this good after a year.

◄◄◄

Keeping Positive

Positive thinking has so many, well, positive effects. Studies have shown that thinking positive is good for your physical health as well, not just for your mental health. Here are some of the main elements of positive thinking:

- ► Flexibility. To be successful, you have to be able to adapt.
- ► Perspective. To get through trials, you need to be able to see all sides of a situation, not just the bad.

▶ Gratitude. It's not about what you don't have or what others have, it's about what you have and what you can share.

▶ Living in the moment. To keep a positive attitude, don't regret the past and don't fret the future. Live in the now. It's the only thing you have any control over.

It's important to keep in mind that no one can be positive all the time, and no one is expecting you to be. It's normal to have moods. You have to feel what's going on, especially when you get sucker-punched by news. You're not going to be in control of your emotions at this point, not when you're not the one in control of that change. You got fired, but you didn't see it coming. Your spouse asked for a divorce, but you didn't see it coming.

A positive perspective is something you get to with time, after you've had time to work through a crisis. It's not the perspective you have when the crisis hits, and that's okay. You're not Pollyanna. You're a human being.

When I tell you to "keep positive," I don't mean you need to lie to yourself about your feelings. It's more about managing your moods and your mood swings, about keeping your moods in check. If you can't be positive, then at least try to be neutral. No one wants to be around a person no one wants to be around.

▶▶

Words From the Wise—Michael Mastro
Broadway Actor/Director/Career Coach

Living in the Moment

Learning to "stay in the moment" and enjoy all aspects of life is an endless journey for me. I hope I'm getting better at it because I believe it's part of what we are here to achieve in this lifetime. Part of what I do to work at these things is to explore different forms of meditation and/or prayer, which I enthusiastically encourage others to do. Whatever your personal spiritual beliefs, there is some form of meditation out there that can work for you.

Another one of my favorite ways to change my emotional state to a positive one is to make a game out of locating things around me and saying to myself about what I see, "I'm grateful for _____ because _____. I'm grateful for _____ because _____."

For instance, while walking in New York City, I might say to myself, "I'm grateful for the sidewalk, because it keeps me safely on my path. I'm grateful for fire hydrants, because they provide water in case of fire. I'm grateful for the air I'm breathing right now, because breathing means I'm alive. I'm grateful for the feeling of the sun on my face, because it gives me hope that spring is finally here," and so forth.

I find it's impossible to do this and not shift my internal energy for the better. It's a great reminder that although I may not be able to control all the circumstances in my life, I can certainly choose how I am going to respond to those circumstances. This "attitude of gratitude" helps to keep me present and leaves less room in my head for "stinking thinking."

◀◀

What "Fuels" You?

Part of having a successful attitude is working on you when you are not around others. It's essential to re-charge. You have to do it daily, if not more often. It's something you need to build into your schedule, just like brushing your hair or flossing.

While you're re-charging, focus on those things that bring you joy and inspiration. Focus on your spirit. You don't have to be religious to have grounding in spiritual guidance. What inspires you? And, as important, how do you make time to drink that in? You can't say, "It doesn't work for me or fit into my schedule." You have to make it work into your schedule.

In order to have the proper grounding for a good, positive, strong attitude that shines off you, you have to begin from within.

Five-Step Decompression Exercise

How do you decompress when you're overwhelmed? Here's a five-step exercise to reset your thinking and de-stress you.

1. Take five deep breaths. Breathe in, count to five, breath out. Repeat.

2. Think of a place you'd rather be, a place that calms you. Don't think of going to the place as an escape, but as an inspiration. It's not a cave; it's a parachute.

3. Take five more deep breaths. Breathe in, count to five, breath out. Repeat.

4. Dream, meditate, and cleanse your brain. What are you doing in that place? What's the thing you most like to do? Think about it. Visualize.

5. Take five more deep breaths. Breathe in, count to five, breath out. Repeat.

The real trick is, once you have decompressed, how can you stay decompressed, and get and stay focused? We discussed getting rid of toxic people in the last chapter, and we'll get more into that in just a bit. We'll also see that toxic people and things aren't the only things that sabotage us.

Get Positive: Quick Fixes

The great thing about positive thinking is that it doesn't take much to set it in motion. If you do these things daily, you'll start feeling better about yourself and your life within a week.

Smile More

Have you ever heard the term "bitchy resting face"? Not everyone has one, but imagine if you had a "smiley resting face"—that your default expression was a smile, not a snarl. I'm not saying you need to sit around grinning like an idiot all the time, but if you make a conscious effort to slightly turn up the corners of your mouth while you're in a meeting or a lecture, waiting in line in the company cafeteria, or just sitting around, you'll not only start to feel happier within yourself, you'll also positively affect others.

Learn to Laugh

Laugh—especially at yourself. Sometimes we goof. Sometimes others like to point out that we goof. And when this happens, we tend to get defensive, and being defensive is a huge element of self-sabotage. What does it help to get defensive? To fold your arms in front of yourself, frown, and make excuses, or worse yet, to place the blame on someone else? Or shoot back at whomever might be calling you on your goof with a goof of theirs (that, most likely, occurred long ago and that you've been storing up for just such an occasion). Instead, diffuse the situation with a laugh.

Watch Yourself

Notice yourself. As you're walking around in the world, catch your reflection in store windows or wherever you can. How do you look? Are you scowling? Smiling? How are you holding your body? Are you slouching? The energy you send out comes back to you. Be aware of the energy you are sending out.

Do Things for Others

There is actual scientific proof that doing things for other people makes you feel better about yourself and the state of the world. Well, maybe it's not exactly scientific, but it's a fairly well-known truth. When you do things for others, it allows you to see outside yourself. If you're suffocating on your own pain, a great way to come up for air from that is to pull outside yourself and get perspective, and focusing on others is a great way to do this. You don't need to have money to be able to give.

For example, I have a good friend, the author Francine LaSala, who recently lost her mother. She felt grief for her loss, but she did not let the situation cripple her. She chose instead to channel her grief into something positive, putting together an anthology of short stories with 18 other authors from around the world, which she published. How was it for others? She made the decision to donate all proceeds from the book to a foundation that does extensive research in the disease that claimed her mother. In addition to benefitting the charity, the book, *A Kind of Mad Courage*, gave 18 other authors a high-profile forum for showcasing their work, and made her feel better about doing something in her mother's memory.

Choose to See the Bright Side

Always remember that the universe is in balance. Every time something terrible happens, you can find a way to turn it around, though not always directly; it doesn't work in a "tit-for-tat" way but, rather, indirectly.

Take Melissa Errico for an example. She had an illness that meant she couldn't sing. As she said in a *Huffington Post* piece on April 21, 2014, "It wasn't just a bump in the road; it was a crushing, heartbreaking bump. The medical problem itself was small, but the impact of leaving the show was greater. I didn't have a foot on land." What happened? She changed her focus for a while. She started a successful blog. She found a way to channel her heartache into something positive, and it's something we can all do.

Keep Track

Remember your journal, where I encouraged you to write about things that you could look forward to each day? That journal is a huge tool in your coming out of self-sabotage and into your own as a functioning, successful, and happy person. Make it a ritual every evening to write down 10 positive things that happened to you over the course of the day, no matter how small they seem, and you will begin to appreciate life and what you have—and have to give—more and more each day. In fact, you could write things down as they happen. The smallest thing matters: You heard a bird chirping. You had the nerve to ask someone a question on the street. You ran one extra mile. You found a quarter!

Get Grounded

It's important to stay positive, but that doesn't mean you need to be delusional. You're not going to get the job simply by manifesting good vibes. You have to be prepared and do the work. Positive thinking, without positive action, gets you nowhere.

Stay Grounded

How do you keep a consistent positive or, at the very least, neutral, attitude in a constantly changing world? How can you keep your perspective and affect the best attitude, even when everything around you threatens to tear you down like a house in a hurricane? How can you stay down-to-earth and relatable even in a position of high power, so your staff sees you not as the czar and the enemy, but as someone leading a team with a common, cooperative goal? You have to keep at it. There's a pervading idea that human beings default to negative thinking as a defense mechanism. If that's the case, then that means humans are predisposed to self-sabotage, which makes it that much more important than not to change your thinking, your attitude, and your perspective.

▶▶

"Why Not?"—Karl duHoffmann
Founder, Orchard Hill Cider Mill

Why me to why not: My story is about both of these things in some ways. I grew up being a dancer. I was a theater person from the time I was five years old. I did musicals; I sang; I danced. My extended family was in the business, and they were mentors to me. My great-uncle, Jon Gregory, was a "groomer" in the Hollywood grooming system. He groomed Fred Astaire, Errol Flynn, Shirley Temple—and so I had old vaudevillian teachers who taught me from the time I was a young kid. I fully planned on becoming a *big* Broadway actor. By the time I got to New York at 16, I was supporting myself by working in commercials. I went into the theater and I had good success there for a long time, though I never quite got to the level I had envisioned. Unemployment is part of the theater, and anytime I was unemployed I worked in restaurants to support my wife and two children.

I learned a lot by working in fine dining in New York City. My philosophy has always been, whatever I'm doing, I want to be fully engaged. I've worked with a lot of actors in restaurants who would say, "I'm not a waiter; I'm an actor." When I was a waiter, I was a waiter, and when I got a job and went off to be an actor, I'd be an actor.

When I opened *Saturday Night Fever*, I had performed on Broadway, and off, for many years. I was so happy to be on Broadway again. However, *Fever* was not a great show and it became more of a job than a rewarding creative undertaking. I started to turn to other activities for a more creatively rewarding experience. That's when I decided to begin exploring the idea of opening my own distillery.

I had been making wine as a hobby with my dad for a while but then we started distilling things. We used apples because New York is a great apple-producing region. Then, a buddy of mine and I set out to open a distillery as a business with the idea of transitioning out of theater. I was still auditioning and doing shows, but I was working on this project on the side. I applied for and received a grant from Career Transitions For Dancers. With that money, I bought barrels and got started!

We met some guys who had just gotten a license upstate for a very small distillery and they let us use their facility. We'd go up on the weekend and eventually I started to bring my products to restaurants I knew to get feedback. This caught the attention of a well-known sommelier that was now working in wine distribution. He recommended me for a brand-management job at his company. It's worked out great for me. I have worked in the business of distribution for years, and currently work for Anchor Distilling.

It has always been a guiding principle of mine that if I was in one place, then I should make the most of that time, even if I would choose to be elsewhere given the opportunity. If I'm spending my time, I don't want to waste it. All the time I was in a restaurant, I never thought, "What am I doing here, waiting on tables? I should be dancing on Broadway." I always looked at it as, "I'm working in a restaurant with a world-famous chef and sommelier," and "This is a great environment full of creative people," and "I want to learn everything about food, wine, and spirits, because my time is too valuable to waste. If I'm going to be here, then I'm going to make the most of it." Curiously enough, that time turned out well-spent and led to opportunities I had never considered.

◄◄

A Positive Perspective

People who think negatively, live negatively; people who think positively, live positively. One of the fundamental laws of the universe is that everything is in balance. To every setback, there's an advantage; to every sorrow, a joy. What determines how you live is what you choose to see and focus on. You can have every advantage in the world, but if you only think about the things you don't have, you're not going to be happy. You can have nothing, and be completely fulfilled and whole.

Depending on how you see the world, this could seem like enlightened thinking or nonsense. What does it sound like to you? (That question isn't rhetorical.)

You make time to use the bathroom. You make time to brush your teeth. Consider this task part of your routine, something you must do every day.

Starting from the last page of your journal, put the date at the top. Now, list numbers going down the page from 1 to 10. Next, think hard and write down on that page 10 things that you don't hate about your life and your career.

Do this every day and you'll start to feel more positive about your life. I'm not saying you're going to snap your fingers and everything will be sunshine and roses and lollipops. Of course, you're going to have bad days, and you're going to struggle. You're human! You're going to get angry, you're going to have to deal with crap, and you're going to feel less than positive sometimes. You're going to get angry at people who tell you to keep positive. That's all okay. Just try, even while you're in the thick of it, to see any 10 things that aren't the worst things in the world. Your perspective will change.

And I guarantee if you were to go the other way with this, listing 10 things that you hate about your life, you'll be depressed in a matter of days. Nothing about your life is different, whether you focus on the positives or the negatives. All of the happenings are still going to happen. But keeping your perspective positive helps you better cope with the highs and the lows.

▶▶▶

"Why Not?"—Catherine Hickland
Theater/Singer/Television Actor/Entrepreneur

A Continual Reinvention

My philosophy is that this is your one and only life. Find your passion and move toward it. If you're no longer passionate about something, find something else.

I never took on anyone else's limitations as my own. People subconsciously project their own lack of ambition and personal fears on us all the time. Even if they don't know they are doing it, people often say things that can hold us back, but it's up to us as to whether or not we believe them. I didn't start singing professionally until I was in my 30s and everyone said it couldn't be done. Telling me I can't do something is like dangling meat in the face of a hungry lion. I had to let them go after I got my first Broadway musical. There will always be people who project on you; the key is to find compassion for them, bless them, and send them on their way.

I always knew what my destiny was and at times my destiny would need to change; I always knew when that was as well. Some people call it a purpose. I call it destiny and following your destiny. My game changer in television was winning the role of Lindsay Rappaport on *One Life to Live*. It changed my career. Even though it was one of many roles I played on television, it was the role that brought me the most notoriety, and playing that bitch was also really a good time.

I haven't found it difficult to transition careers because rarely does it occur to me that I can't do something—that's not how I'm wired. Of course, I've fallen down, had some hard knocks and big scrapes. But I train myself to look at obstacles as opportunities to grow. And though I still feel fear, I don't let it hold me back. I use it to move forward, asking myself, "What's stronger—my fear or my desire?"

I have always done my own makeup for shows and, like most girls, I'm a makeup junkie. What started as a hobby eventually led to a full-blown business. In 2001, I launched Cat Cosmetics because I absolutely believed I could make a better product than what was available. I discovered that as an entrepreneur, you work your ass off and do not sleep for the first five years. I have such respect for people who start their own businesses, especially women. Being an actor is easy compared to managing people and a company. That being said, it brings me great joy and I have a very successful business. My mother-in-law, Debbie Reynolds, always says, "Give the people what they want," and I agree. I listen to what they want and then I give it to them.

I also teach a two-day seminar called "Get Your Fire Back," which helps people get excited about their lives by teaching them about emotional vampires and how to rid their lives of them, how to look 10 years younger in less than five minutes, how to have fun, and how to get people to say "yes" by using four simple words. It's so rewarding to see people shed what holds them back and just "become" themselves right in front of your eyes.

And I teach stage hypnosis to help people break free of stage fright and gain confidence by "doing." I've been interested in hypnosis since I was young, and I finally studied it during the evenings while I was doing *One Life to Live*. At the time, I was writing my book, *The 30-Day Heartbreak Cure*, and I wanted to have the educational backing to support my material. I never imagined I would be doing hypnosis as a career, but now I do over 200 shows a year—and I'm still teaching.

If you are doing something you loathe doing, you will not have the time, energy, or attitude to do what you love or plan your way out of where you are. That is my balance. I have made career moves that people thought I would deeply regret, but what they didn't understand was that I had no passion for it anymore. My philosophy is that this is your one and only life. Find your passion and move toward it.

◀◀

You Are What You Project

If your reputation precedes you, your attitude defines you. Although none of us is ever as transparent as our fear makes us believe we are, our general attitude is something that's obvious the minute we walk into a room.

If you're feeling under confident, it will show unless you take steps to turn that around. If you're feeling overly cocky, it will show unless you take steps to turn that around. You don't want to be too full of anything, especially yourself, whether in a good or bad way. Be conscious. Stay grounded. Focus.

It may surprise you to know that most people, when faced with the prospect of entering a room full of strangers at a cocktail party, feel nervous and apprehensive about having to reach out and speak to all those people they don't know. Then why isn't everyone hovering in the corner or around the buffet table? Attitude!

It may also surprise you that even the top performers will admit to having stage fright just before hitting the stage. But it never shows (with top performers). Why? Attitude!

It may equally surprise you that that guy Frank in marketing, who gives the killer presentations and has clients eating out of the palm of his hand each time he presents, struggles with a stutter. Or that Eve, who just got promoted to the executive level in the accounting department, sometimes struggles with math. People succeed and overcome, no matter what they've been given, because they don't allow what they've been given to be what defines them. Instead, they know what it's about and how to use what they do have to climb toward their goals. It's all about attitude!

The right attitude, connected to your strategy, aligned with your ambition, can set your life on fire.

There was a young film school graduate, Mike, who had worked for a year for a famous film maker as an assistant camera operator. When the work was available, it was rewarding and thrilling. But there were long droughts after a film was completed. So he started looking for new work. He saw an ad online from a world class optical technology company, which stated that only candidates with five years of experience would be considered. Mike only had two years, and no direct experience, but he submitted his resume anyway.

He got rejected, and he submitted it again. He got rejected again, and then submitted it again. This piqued the curiosity of the HR manager who invited him to their headquarters. The HR manager was flabbergasted at how confident, knowledgeable, articulate, and grounded Mike was for a young guy of 24; they hired him.

I had the opportunity of coaching Mike for an industry trade show soon after he was hired. After spending an hour with him I told him, "You are a star, and you will be promoted within six months. I'm just sure of it."

The following year I was invited back to coach other spokespeople and Mike walked into the room to see me. He said, "I just want you to know you were right. I got promoted within six months." He wasn't conceited about it; he was excited and proud, but never took it for granted. That, my friend, is star quality.

Charisma Is Key

Speaking of star quality, do you want to know a great checkpoint for your attitude being well-adjusted? It's charisma. Charisma is that intangible quality a person has to be able to light up the room simply because. Well, charisma is not fairy dust. It's not magic. Though some people may naturally possess more charisma than others, that doesn't mean you can't affect it in your attitude.

Think about what makes for a charismatic person. He or she seems to know that he or she is something—is someone. That sense creates a sort of aura around that person. Waves seem to vibrate off of him or her, waves that draw others in. We want to follow that energy, even if we don't quite always understand at the moment why we do.

There isn't any pill you can swallow to give you the charisma of someone like Bill Clinton, but you can work to affect it as part of your attitude adjustment. Remember that charisma is about being in the moment, about clearly enjoying what you're doing and having a great time at it. It's about clearly enjoying the people around you and letting them know (or at least believe) that you are listening, and that in this moment, the only thing in the world that matters are the words coming out of the other person's mouth.

Can you pretend to listen? Of course you can. Pretend to do anything long enough, and you'll find yourself actually doing it—like smiling. Make yourself smile for a while and you'll be smiling.

Successful CEOs and other C-Suite executives listen all the time. The best CEOs listen and have found techniques to keep them focused. They keep refreshing themselves. They work to draw out information.

How can you practice listening? Here are some pointers:

- ▶ Make eye contact. Don't just look at a person when they're speaking to you; look into them.
- ▶ Ask questions. The best way for people to know that you are listening is if you ask pointed questions about what they're saying that help draw out more than "yes" and "no" answers.

- ▶ Nod. It takes no effort to do and is a huge, nonverbal acknowledgment that you hear and understand what's being said to you. Just don't become a bobble-head doll nodding at every word. That's not listening, that's a physical tic.

- ▶ Repeat. Especially if someone seems particularly excited about what they're sharing with you. Use phrases like, "So what you're saying is...." and "Do I understand correctly that...?"

- ▶ Don't look away. It's really easy at an event to get distracted by all the buzz in the room, but remember how important it is to make this person believe they are the only person in the universe at that moment. Look at that person for as long as they are trying to engage you and don't look away. Don't smirk. Think of a pleasant experience that brings a smile to your face—your child, your pet—and hold that smile a second or two longer than feels natural. Though not a second longer than that as you don't want to come off as leering or creepy!

- ▶ Find something you can genuinely compliment them on. There's always something, even with the hottest messes. It's a short statement: "You look lovely in blue," or "That's a nice necklace." Don't overdo it.

▶▶

Words From the Wise—Michael James Scott
Broadway Musical Theater Actor/Singer/Dancer

Working It

I feel like people try too hard to have charisma, but I don't think it's something that can be taught. It comes from within. I do believe, however, that you can teach someone to be gracious, and that trait will naturally bring out charismatic action, which may be seen as charisma. Someone with confidence usually has a charisma about them that draws you in, and I think there's a great deal to learn from that. Confidence and graciousness will bring a natural sense of charisma.

I think appearing to be effortless onstage is something that comes from a place of trust within yourself. You can do all the training in the world, and research and master techniques, but the minute you start to second-guess yourself, there begins a huge avalanche of doubt that is hard to escape.

I think nerves are good—it's the way you choose to use them that makes the difference. Nerves push us to be on our gig in the best possible way. We are our hardest critics, so when you can use nerves and channel them in a positive way, it can be quite fulfilling in the moment.

I personally like to incorporate the use of faith. It's not a religious thing as it's about having faith within yourself to tackle whatever you're doing in a way that assures you that, not only do you trust the work you've done to prepare yourself, but that you actually have faith in everything you've done leading up to that big moment. It's a beautiful thing to be able to have that faith. To leave the doubt behind and actually focus on the fact that there's nothing left to do but go out and perform.

◀◀

Bottom Line

It's never too late to get your attitude in check and start projecting into the world the image of a confident (not cocky or steam-roller-ish), capable, and focused person who is not only "up to the task," but one who's ready, willing, and fully able to nail that task and take on whatever else is needed. Sometimes it's all about attitude.

4

Focus

You can't depend on your eyes when your imagination is out of focus.
—Mark Twain

We live in a world of distractions, no doubt about it. There's a flurry of activity flitting around us all the time. During the day, we feel obligated to multitask in everything we do in order to get everything done. In fact, even in our quietest hours, there's "noise." How many of us find ourselves looking at Facebook, reading through e-mail, or scrolling through our Twitter feeds at night in bed, after already spending so much time behind a screen during the day? When pillow talk means sending an e-mail to your colleague, you know you're in trouble.

Where's the time built in to take a breath, clear our minds, chill out, and dream? We don't take that time, but we need it—*desperately.*

Without it, we aren't able to step back and get clarity on our lives; we're not able to strategize about what we need to get done and the course we'd like for our lives to take. If we never have time to think about what needs doing, to get where we want to get going, we'll never get there.

A life without downtime is a life of self-sabotage. A life without structure is a life of self-sabotage. A life without organization of things, time, ideas, and dreams is a life of self-sabotage. In this chapter, I'll introduce you to some people who have learned how to focus away from distractions and focus on finding success. I'm also going to show you how to stay flexible and adapt to change as it arises. Because change always arises, and your strategy for success depends on your ability to bend off the course of your plan when the situation calls for it.

The Disaster of Distraction

Because I'm a public speaker and a performer, I need to stay fit and look as good as I possibly can. My appearance is very important, especially considering how important first impressions are (more on this in Chapter 5).

One night, when I was under a great deal of pressure due to travel and work projects, I was incredibly distracted, my mind all a flutter with the myriad details about booking travel, researching my clients' needs, and packing for an overseas trip.

On my way home that night, I bought a salad, brought it into my kitchen, and mindlessly opened the silverware drawer to remove a fork, which I placed on the counter. It seems that my housekeeper had found a random magnet that day, from where I don't know, and had left it on the kitchen counter for me to examine. Unbeknownst to me, because I didn't know the magnet was there, the fork connected with the magnet.

My mind on my own thoughts, I put on the evening news, picked up the fork, dug into the salad, and took a big bite. Snap! From biting into lettuce (I thought) one of my upper front teeth broke off all the way to the top! On lettuce! Was I that old?!

It was only then that I examined the fork and found the real culprit: a one-inch black magnet stuck to the fork. Had I been paying attention to the task at hand, preparing and eating my dinner, I probably would have noticed a one-inch black magnet sticking to the back of my fork! But I wasn't concentrating in the moment. Instead, I was "checking in at the airport" and "landing overseas" and "claiming my baggage" and "checking in to my hotel"—all of these things happening in the future, not in the moment. And for that, I got burned.

▶▶

Words From the Wise—Karla Visconti
*Director, Corporate Communications Caribbean
and Latin America for Hilton Worldwide*

Be More than Prepared
I help spokespeople stay focused on their messages. The key to staying focused on your message is to be prepared.

In preparation, it's important to look at the big picture, consider all the moving parts and make sure you have each piece covered, and then apply this when creating a strategy and setting objectives.

There is an enthusiasm that comes along with being in a fast-paced environment, especially when the objectives set are clear and achieved. In my experience, I've learned it's a good strategy to give people the information they need and position my expectations accordingly. For example, if I need an executive to provide a quote for a story, I present a drafted response that he or she can simply review and approve.

To keep focused and be successful, it's important to prepare and be flexible. Prepare yourself for what you want, do research and engage in development opportunities to educate yourself, stay current on trends in the chosen field, and then be flexible to adapt to changes in the field.

◀◀

The Cycle of Self-Sabotage

I have helped numerous companies navigate crises and I've developed a tool to show employees and executives alike how to anticipate a crisis before it could happen, to focus on the warning signs in order to avert catastrophe. These signs also work very well in understanding self-sabotage. So here I'm going to show you how to avert crises by using these markers with, as an example, my own self-sabotage story of the magnet that stole my tooth.

How many of us really love to go to the dentist? I would bet less than 1 percent of the worldwide population, which makes it a great way to help detail the cycle of self-sabotage:

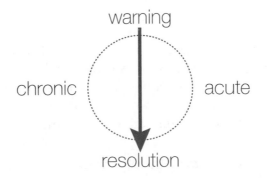

The idea is to examine Warning signs and go straight to Resolution, before the situation goes into Crisis Mode—Acute. And, naturally, to get things well under control before they become Chronic.

Back to my story: I had but a few days before I had to leave the country for work. I hate going to the dentist, but I had no choice but to try and get an emergency appointment. How many people are going to take serious, life-changing advice from a toothless speaker?

I have a bit of a phobia about dentists in general due to a rather brutal experience I had with my dentist when I was growing up. He was rough and I always left feeling a little bruised. I didn't know there were more gentle dentists.

When I got older, I found a dentist who is not the warmest guy, and could also be somewhat intimidating, but it was nothing like the sadist I went to when I was a kid in Denver, so I stayed with him. What did I know? I never had real problems with my teeth so I kept myself stuck in the status quo.

When I moved away from that area and into Manhattan, I told myself it was time to find a new dentist, someone more local. But I kept putting it off—in part because there's something to be said for sticking with "the devil you know" and also because I was busy. I was too distracted with other things to bother. It was easier maintaining the status quo.

Warning

There were numerous reasons to seek out a new dentist. The "Warning" was there. The two-hour drive to and from the suburbs was a drag. The office staff was not terribly gracious, and I always felt I was being sent to the principal's office when I made an appointment. The experience was unpleasant, even for going to the dentist, but I ignored all the warning signs.

Acute

Then the magnet episode happened. The crisis! I had to drive up in a state of emergency, because I was to travel soon and it's just a teeny bit difficult to be a compelling public speaker when you have a snaggle front tooth and look like a miner from an old western movie. I was angry with myself for not paying attention to details and now this situation.

I stopped for coffee on the way to the appointment to try and calm down, and I was so distracted, I lost my iPhone.

I arrived at the office to find the dentist was, as usual with me, not in a good mood. He scares me. I never feel comfortable asking him questions. And now he is proceeding to tell me that this was going to be a "very big job" and "a burden for him." I'm in a crisis of my own doing, and the situation seems to be getting worse, not better, as he jabs away at my snaggle tooth and fits a really hideous temporary front tooth over the newly-built pin drilled into my gum.

I had my business trip and felt self-conscious all the while. Did I make a good impression? You bet I didn't, and it probably had less to do with the look of my mouth than my nerves over how my mouth looked—that all eyes were on my bad tooth!

After the trip, I'm back in the guy's office again, and he's scolding me while he's drilling me. I suddenly felt I was Dustin Hoffman in the movie *Marathon Man*. I think, now is the time to find a new dentist! Except that I'd already paid him a considerable fee and convinced myself I needed to see it through.

I was so upset over all of it on the way home that I rear-ended another car.

Resolution

At this writing, I as yet have no permanent front tooth so I still need to go back. I will, after this event, find a new dentist in Manhattan. But if I don't make a change, I'm stuck. This will make the situation *Chronic*.

Most of this could have been resolved by my simply finding a new dentist when I moved to Manhattan. Plenty of people have given me recommendations but I procrastinated. I avoided dealing with the issue. I was too busy to get my act together on it. And for that, I paid (and paid, and paid, and paid).

An unfocused mind is a forgetful mind. An unfocused mind is not only self-sabotage, it can lead to disaster. For me, it led to, first, a broken tooth, then stress, then a car accident—a minor one, but it could have been far worse than a fender-bender.

Unfortunately, an unfocused mind forced me to go to a place I never want to be: first the dentist; then on the phone with my insurance company.

▶▶▶

Words From the Wise—Laureen Cook
Principal TMT Advisor, IFC (World Bank), Telecommunications, Media, and Technology Investment Sector

Know Your Audience; Trust Your Instincts
If you've done your homework and are culturally astute, you need to remember to trust your instincts when maneuvering through a new multi-cultural working environment. As long as I am well prepared, I focus on the end goal and don't dwell on what other people may think. You have to adopt the ability to filter out the noise so that you do not get distracted and remain focused on the objective of the meeting. I understand that this is hard for many people to do, but it's something that you have to become good at doing while working in a culture not of your own: compartmentalizing and prioritizing.

Whether it's about a new technology or a new country, I do my homework. Because I am not a linguist, I research the cultural norms and learn a few words of the local language in order to grasp some of the nuances of the culture. The way of working with people from the UK is very different from the way of working with people from Germany, or people from various countries in the Middle East, Asia, Africa, or Latin America.

◀◀◀

Getting Your Act Together

We all could use a good daily dose of "getting our act together." In this world, it's really easy to come off looking flakey and ineffective, even when you're juggling multiple tasks.

As with any plan, there needs to be flexibility, but there has to be a common groundwork that we stick to. Otherwise, things rapidly start to flail out of our control. As Julliard does next, creating a schedule, even a loose one, can help us manage our time and properly focus on those things that need to be done when it's their time to be done.

Whether trying to get a handle on a humongous project, grappling with a job and family, just a huge, all-consuming job, or a huge, all-consuming family, having a grounding like a schedule and a plan for execution (your tasks, not your colleagues and/or loved ones) really helps keep things in check.

▶▶▶

Words From the Wise—Laurence Julliard
Corporate Executive/Entrepreneur/Owner, French Pension

Schedule Your Life
I have organized my days to allow all the critical things to be done.

Mondays I go to the Geneva office, unless something happens to one of the kids. This is my day in the office. They go to the daycare in the morning and after school, and I always have back up with friends to go pick them up if I have a late meeting. In the office, I spend my day exchanging with the team.

Tuesdays are my project day, so I go to the office to work on my projects, but that day I always leave early to pick up the kids at 4 p.m. and engage with them—then, homework, bath, and dinner.

Wednesdays are kids' days! They come first. If I have work to get done, I do it early in the morning or when I am waiting for them (during dance class or tennis lesson). We usually do something fun in the afternoon—I plan a different activity each week. And sometimes we just decide to do nothing and we read books in front of the fire.

Thursdays I work from home and this is when I get all my thinking done.

Friday morning I spend time at the city hall and Friday afternoon at the hotel to get everything organized for the hotel (asset management, food management, planning, and HR issues).

On the weekend, my husband and I alternate between serving at the hotel/restaurant/bar and being with the kids.

Every morning, I spend one to two hours at the hotel to prepare for the day and serve breakfast, usually between 6:30 and 8:30 a.m.

Every night, I spend an hour doing accounting and invoicing, and we review everything on the weekend.

Sunday afternoon is family time.

◀◀◀

Scheduling and Making Lists

Scheduling can be tedious, and it's the kind of thing people like to avoid, but as we have demonstrated already in this chapter, it's the kind of thing that will mean some small suffering upfront to avoid much larger suffering down the line.

You can schedule on your computer or phone, which means you can get electronic prompts when it's time to do something or go somewhere. These reminders are handy and automatic, and therefore recommended. Except I'm going to recommend that you not make your phone or your computer your "go to" scheduling source.

Remember earlier on, when we discussed the science of writing, of actually writing something down? It becomes really effective when it comes to plotting and organizing tasks. Not only is information about what you're recording further enforced by the act of actually writing it down, you'll be able to see more of your schedule at a glance and to change it more easily and dramatically if it exists as a white board, with different colored inks, that hangs in a prominent place in your life. Maybe it's your kitchen, maybe it's your cubicle wall.

Wherever you decide to place it, the keyword here is "prominent." If other people are going to be relying on it as well, make sure it is accessible. If someone else needs to see what happens when, it's only fair that the schedule is visible to that other person. (That doesn't mean you need to make writing implements or erasers accessible to anyone else. The last thing you need is people changing all the scheduling at will!)

Also, make lists. Aside from schedules, this is your most crucial tool for staying organized and keeping focused. As discussed earlier, you should not have one list where you put down anything and everything you need to do in your life. This will make you nuts! This is a list you will never be able to complete or even complete compiling. Make one list of daily goals, one of weekly goals, and one of monthly goals.

As you plot and plan and schedule, be sure you leave yourself breathing room in between tasks and appointments. You do not want to over-schedule yourself for many reasons, including that it's nuts to make yourself nuts, but also, it's generally always better to be early than to be late. You don't want the stress of not being able to make your next appointment because the one you're at is running long.

If you have extra time, that's great! Don't think of this as wasted time; think of it as breathing time. This is when you can do the exercises we've been talking about, like the Five-Step Decompression Exercise. Clear your mind, relax, meditate, dream.

▶▶▶

Words From the Wise—Kevin B. McGlynn
International Musical Theater Performer

Relax, Refocus

For someone like me who is constantly traveling, I use a lot of personal and private methods for relaxation. I guess you could call it meditation. I sit quietly by myself, focus on the job at hand, and visualize step by step how that will be achieved. I see it happening in my mind's eye. It's a game plan I use as a basis from which I can deviate or elaborate, depending on what's happening in the moment.

Inhale pink; exhale blue. That's what I always say to myself before going into an audition or at the beginning of a show. It's my way of stepping into the moment, of leaving the real world behind and releasing any nerves or negative energy. The same way a cold plate is the enemy of a hot meal, so are the nerves to a performer.

I believe relaxation and focus are essential tools to give your best performance, and that you need to have your feet firmly planted on the ground and not be inside your own head, especially in an audition situation where you may only have seconds to get yourself to the right emotional level of a character's song.

◄◄◄

De-Cluttering

Out with the old and in with the new. I talked about this in Chapter 2, but I want to reinforce it here because being in an uncluttered space is conducive to bringing in fresh thought and clear ideas. I believe you cannot reinvent until you de-clutter.

As we talked about in the first part of this book, letting go can be painful. It can be the hardest thing in the world, but it can also be cleansing. You don't have to throw things away. Give them to consignment shops and you could make some money. There are great shops all over the U.S. and wonderful online sources. Work with a SPARC buddy to help you decide what stays and what goes.

Hoarding is about being stuck in a place, and reinvention is about breaking out of a place and into a new way of thinking. In order to have the psychic space to reinvent, you have to de-clutter.

By the way, this isn't just about those tangible things you trip over in the hallway. De-cluttering also means taking a good hard look at your computer and making sure it's uncluttered and organized:

▶ Do not save files on your desktop. Not only does this soon start to look like a patchwork of random madness, it's also not a safe place for your files to live.

▶ Do build systems of folders and use them. Don't get lazy. Start with "Documents" and create a hierarchy of files so you'll always know where files are. Create a "Documents" folder and in it folder for "Home" and "Work." In the "Home" folder, perhaps have more folders broken down by "Bills," "Address Lists," and so forth. And in the "Work" folder, perhaps more folders broken down by "Invoices," "Proposals," "Memos," and so forth.

The same goes for your e-mail. Every e-mail program gives you the ability to organize your messages into files. Use these files! If you have a client who e-mails you regularly, that client gets his or her own file. If there are numerous complicated projects you do for that client, consider breaking down your folders that way.

Get in the habit that every time you open an e-mail, you read it and then you either delete it immediately or you place it in a designated folder. If you don't regularly order from a vendor who e-mails you daily, unsubscribe. After a while, there isn't much of anything worthwhile that comes from solicitation e-mails. It's all just noise. Do yourself a favor and only subscribe to e-mails that directly and daily matter to you.

There are many books on organizing and de-cluttering out there, as well as hundreds of Websites that can show you how to get your computer files organized in a system really customized to suit your needs. You need to find that system; I can't create it for you. All I can do here is show you how you can begin to feel less overwhelmed and more on top of your day.

Finances

Although we work to live (even though some may brag that they live to work), we don't always see being organized with our finances as a way to bring clarity and focus into our daily lives—professional or otherwise. But we should.

When your money is under control and being handled responsibly, it not only frees you up to not worry about money, it also buys you freedom to start exploring what your options could be if you didn't have the current job you have, at the salary you're making. It allows you to see how much money you need to live, and how much more you might need to live differently.

No matter your age, find a financial advisor you can trust, but do your own investment research as well. Always have checks and balances. Don't allow any one person to have total control over your money.

▶▶▶

Words From the Wise—Lee Koenigsberg, MBA
Financial Advisor

Taking Charge of Your Finances

Everyone should have a will, a power of attorney, and a health proxy. Even a young, single person with inconsequential assets may suffer a medical crisis (health proxy), a severe disabling event (power of attorney), or premature death (will). These documents give us total control as to who will handle matters if any of these misfortunes were to occur. All of these documents need to be reviewed periodically to: 1) reflect changes in our own lives (marriage, birth of a child) and 2) the continued suitability of the people named in these documents who are expected to act on our behalf.

We may think that once we finally landed a decent-paying job, we can totally indulge ourselves; after all, we deserve it: an apartment that might be more expensive than is prudent, an extensive, fashionable wardrobe, frequent restaurant/bar tabs, and so forth. Even if there were some assurance that this "gravy train" of a good salary were to continue (an unlikely scenario), the concession to instant gratification comes with a steep price.

The two important universal goals that should be included on everyone's list are 1) an emergency fund and 2) retirement.

The emergency fund is a reserve that is available in case one loses his/her job or suffers some sort of catastrophic financial setback. The fund should be able to cover all living expenses for a period of three to six months (depending on which financial maven one listens to). This fund should be invested conservatively.

And, finally, time to talk about retirement. Although there is a trend for some people to forego the traditional retirement age and keep working, the likelihood is that each of us will need to rely on a nest egg if/when we stop working (particularly if one might find themselves involuntarily retired by their employer).

◀◀◀

Focusing Around Others

There are two things to be considered here. The first is how you keep yourself focused in a world where it seems everyone else's job is to throw you off—off-track, off-balance, off-schedule—and also try and bring them under your "focusing" wing.

I joke when I bring families into this, because it isn't always your kids that are trying to throw you off. Sometimes it's your staff, sometimes your manager. Sometimes it's a person behind the counter or on the other end of the line when you call for customer-service, or any number of situations. Whatever the case, *focus* can help you navigate around it.

▶▶▶

Words From the Wise—Cheryl Raymond
Manager Public Programs and Special Events, New York Public Library for the Performing Arts at Lincoln Center

Navigating Bureaucracy
In my 35 years of working for a major non-profit institution, I have used the following techniques to get successful results:

1. I listen to and recognize my support staff and all that they do to help make a successful event.

2. I have remembered that sometimes you get better results going through the back door than in the front.

3. I have kept up with technology to improve my work and have taken advantage of any professional development and training opportunities my company has offered.

4. I have been organized and have communicated not only with the staff that works directly with me, but with those who work with them as well.

Dealing with the public is not always easy. A friendly smile and the words "please" and "thank you" go a long way.

◀◀◀

Focusing to Influence Others

The second thing to consider is how you can use your focus to influence others—though not your subordinates or your partner or your children—to get people to do what you want them to do.

I have a great anecdote I love to share when it comes to this. I met Karen Radwin, executive director of the American Cancer Society's Hope Lodge Program, a few years back at a fundraiser. During the event, gently worn clothes were being auctioned, with proceeds to benefit Hope Lodge.

I noticed a woman walk by wearing a beautiful black sequined jacket, and I mentioned in passing how nice I thought it was. Several minutes later, Karen approached me, holding that sequined black jacket over her arm, a price tag dangling from the sleeve. I was stunned. Karen said, "Here's your new jacket."

This was an exquisite display of focus. Although she was at the party, casually conversing, she was also highly focused, paying attention to what people were wanting, and strategizing how to get it for them, all while benefitting the cause.

Focus is about keeping your eyes open. It's about seeing opportunities beyond the moment you're currently in, while staying in the moment. It's about taking calculated risks and putting all the pieces together. It takes a clear mind to do this, but it's an amazing and powerful skill worth mastering. You have to first be able to size up your audience, and then know what show you need to put on for them.

Remember, there's no business like show business, and all business is "show."

▶▶▶

Words From the Wise—Karen Radwin
Executive Director, American Cancer Society's
Hope Lodge Program in NY/NJ

Getting What You Want in Spite of Others

Egos and personalities can get in the way of progress. Though it takes work, I have found that bearing the responsibility for controlling your own ego can earn you points with others. If you focus on what is important and keep your ego in check, others will soften eventually and there will be mutual success.

In terms of helping others overcome obstacles, I believe the facilitator hat a manager wears is important. Managers are traffic cops and problem solvers. I have had to facilitate situations where two sides are not working well together. In such cases, I have brought the sides together to get a sense of the problem and the dynamic, and then met with each side independently to identify what is truly at the heart of the issues they are having. When you peel away the layers and get to the center, you gain an understanding of what each side truly needs. From that point, you work long and hard to breach the gap between the parties. It takes commitment on the part of all parties, but if everyone is willing to make the effort, you see results. At some point, you are able to determine if one of the parties is merely giving lip service. In those cases, you have to cut your losses and deal with the situation differently and quickly.

We all have red tape in our lives; the key is to understand the processes that a company or organization has. I think we oftentimes believe that taking a shortcut will get us to our destination faster than following the road map our environment has in place. When that happens, we really do get stuck and end up having to invest the time we should have taken initially to follow the process.

Here are my five tips for getting your project focused:

1. Know the "What" and the "Why"—You need to have solid justification for taking on a project. Do your homework. Get all the facts before you get started.

2. Engage the "Who"—Select the right people whose expertise and talents will complement the work that has to be done.

3. Establish the "How" and "When"—Set down ground rules of behavior for effort for the project, involving everything from timelines and agendas to what is expected in terms of trust and respect for other team members.

4. Step Away; Simmer—When you think you have it all figured out, give yourself some distance and then revisit. Some gentle tweaking can go a long way.

5. Enjoy the Journey—Part of what makes for a satisfying end result is enjoying how you got there. Make note of the parts of the process that were particularly enjoyable, as well as those that were not, and use those findings to inform your next project.

◀◀

SPARC-ing Focus

Yes, your SPARC buddy comes in handy for everything! Remember when I told you that you're driving the car on your journey, and that your SPARC buddy is holding the map? This is so essential when it comes to *focus*, because who better to spark you to focus than a SPARC buddy?

Work with your SPARC buddy to help you navigate your journey. Concentrate on these points:

► Strategy. What do you need to hone in on? Make a list of five different elements in your life that need your attention. Share your list with your buddy.

► Purpose. Why these elements above all others? Have three reasons. Be as specific as possible.

► Analyze. What are your hopes and dreams for these elements? What do you hope to achieve?

► Rehearse. Have your SPARC buddy go over your plan with you and walk you through your strategy a few times, brainstorming, and locating where potential "land mines" (people, scheduling conflicts) could trip you up as you focus in on what needs to be done.

► Commit. Have your SPARC buddy keep "looking over your shoulder" so to speak, to make sure you're staying on track and staying "in the now."

Remember that one of the main keys of focus is to concentrate on the *now*.

▶▶▶

Words From the Wise—Merri Sugarman
Casting Director, Tara Rubin Casting in New York

Focus on the "Now"

When I screen actors, I really try to create an atmosphere that's supportive and warm so people can do their best work. Marrying art and commerce is always the biggest challenge. I don't always know if actors will be directable; I can ask them to make adjustments and get an idea of how they listen and call on their skills and technique to make changes smartly and quickly. But the truth is that you never know until you're into the rehearsal process what an actor is capable of—emotionally, physically, and behaviorally.

My advice for being interviewed: try not to dwell on what it is you think we are looking for. You'll never figure it out or be 100 percent correct. Concentrate on showing what it is that you bring to the table—why you shine. In the end, you may be the right fit. Or, you may not be right, not for this job or this moment, but if you "show" well, you'll be remembered positively. Whether you get booked or not, that can only mean good things are coming in the future. This could be a job, a referral, or a recommendation later.

Also, try not to do too much chatting. It diffuses focus and energy. You have to exist in the moment. I appreciate people who are ready to get down to it and confident and excited to show what makes them special.

◀◀◀

Bottom Line

You lose a lot of time and expend a lot of energy unnecessarily when you're operating your life out of focus. There are always going to be distractions and "noise" vying for your attention and trying to sabotage your efforts, but you can train yourself to move beyond that and start expending your energy into pursuits that will move you off the hamster wheel and into the main playing field.

5

Appearance

Nothing succeeds like the appearance of success.
—Christopher Lasch

She shuffled into the room alone and quietly took a seat in the back row, for the most part looking down at her shoes. She had on a red satin top that looked like it might have been pulled from her roommate's closet and a pencil skirt that hugged her curves just a bit too snugly.

Her clothes spoke flashy confidence, but her demeanor was nothing like that. Instead of walking up to anyone with a greeting as bold as the blouse she wore, she sat by herself. After a few minutes, she headed to the buffet table where others clustered in easy conversation. She slipped through the crowds, placed a sandwich on her plate, and headed right back to her seat.

Although the woman was unnoticed by most others in the group, she intrigued me. She wasn't the typical type of person to come to a networking seminar—not quite a social dynamo—and I had to know why she was here, to help her get something out of it.

I introduced myself to her and started to make small talk. She nodded and murmured in reply. I asked her about the color red, if it was a favorite of hers, and she looked at me like she couldn't imagine why I was asking. Then she crossed her arms over her shirt.

"Louise," I began, "Tell me what you're hoping to take away from this seminar."

"Well," she replied, "I'd really like to find a new job, so I was hoping to make some connections. You know, network?"

Her smile was warm and sincere. I was compelled to help her. "So how do you think you're going to make those connections sitting all the way back here?"

That smile again. "I'm kind of scared to talk to people I don't know. I guess I've just always been really shy," she said, and she crossed her arms over her shirt again.

Instead of waiting for the irony of trying to remain anonymous at a networking event to dawn on her, I gave her a nudge. The more I spoke with her, and the more she opened up to me, the more it was obvious that Louise was a classic example of a person walking around without any sense of brand—who maybe read a book that told her how to dress to stand out at a social function and was now wearing an outfit that made her feel even more self-conscious and withdrawn than she was.

In our short conversation, I learned that she hated being the center of attention, but that she loved helping others, that she really enjoyed being part of a winning team, but that she never needed any credit for what she did.

She was in dire need of a makeover and she had no idea. She was uncomfortable in her clothes, but there was way more to it than that. The way she carried herself, the way she held her body—the signs were everywhere that she wasn't feeling her appearance was up to par, underconfidence on the inside seeping its way out. She knew she wasn't presenting herself in the best possible way, but she didn't know where to begin to fix it.

Louise is not alone. Most people are walking around oblivious about how they look and sabotaging themselves every step of the way. The good news is that the more you grow from inside (as you develop from saboteur to success with what you'll learn in this book), the more you'll flower on the outside.

Appearance is important for so many reasons. Everything is wrapped up in your wrapping. In this chapter, I'll walk you through the essential elements of appearance and I'll coach you to figure out if what you're putting out there for everyone to see is helping or hurting you.

Let Your SPARC Buddy Help You "SPARC"-le!

It's easier to speak to someone about their sexual proclivities than it is about their appearance. That's why it's especially important to have a

SPARC buddy who not only has a sense of style, but also a sense of compassion when it comes to your appearance.

Though you may be sensitive and feel attacked by criticism that focuses on how you look and carry yourself, try and keep an open mind here! Remember, you chose your SPARC buddy (or buddies) because you want them to be open with you. This is a person (or people) who is only looking out for you, and who you feel will deliver the information you need to hear in a kind and constructive way.

Look, everyone has figure faults. But what we don't always see are our attributes. It's not a SPARC buddy's job to point out those faults, but to help you see those parts of you that look nice. For the rest of this chapter, we'll go through the elements we touched on here.

▶▶▶

Words From the Wise—
Dr. Katherine Mastrota, MS, OD, FAAO
Center Director, Omni Eye Surgery

A Stitch in Time Saves Nine

Visual hygiene is important particularly with extended close work or computer usage. Regular breaks from near focus, proper ergonomics, and lighting as well as the proper working distance and eyeglass prescription can reduce fatigue, headaches, and eye strain associated with these tasks. It is also key to maintain a near-normal blink rate as intense near work/computer usage tends to reduce the blink rate leading to ocular surface drying and discomfort.

Take a break from your computer every 20 minutes. You can even download a "blinker" for your screen to remind you!

It makes sense that if we are suffering from dehydration, so too will our ocular surface. I recommend to my patients to be mindful of fluid consumption and suggest increasing (appropriately) such if it seems inadequate.

Small yet important changes may be instrumental in delaying or preventing the negative changes in ocular surface as it responds to age, environment, disease, and contact lens–wear. Think ahead.

◀◀◀

At the Core

Appearance is about hair and skin and clothing, but before that, it's really about your "core." This is the part of you that holds the rest of you together—the trunk of your tree, with your arms, legs, head, and neck as the branches. If this isn't working, most anything else won't. Fitness is your friend here. Having a strong core relies on strength training, which we'll talk more about later in this chapter.

Posture is probably the most important aspect of your appearance that depends on your core. So many people are walking around with terrible posture, and it speaks volumes about their ability to achieve success. When your shoulders hunch forward, you immediately look underconfident. It doesn't matter how confident you may feel; your bad posture shouts out to others "I can't handle this" and "I can't do this" and "Please don't notice me; I'm the worst." These are not messages you want to relay to potential clients or employers—or even romantic partners! You have to improve your posture. Here's how.

I want you now to stand in front of a full-length mirror. I never knew until recently how many people don't even own a full-length mirror, which seems crazy to me. I actually believe that viewing yourself in a three-way mirror, so you can see all sides of you, is the best way to view yourself, as this is the way others will see you. But most of us don't have the kind of room in our homes to install three-way mirrors.

In any case, while you're standing in front of that mirror, so you can see yourself from the side, I want you to put your weight a little forward so you're on the balls of your feet, but keeping your heels firmly planted for stability. You'll know if you're standing correctly if you ask a friend to try to push you off balance. If you falter, you're not balancing your weight correctly.

Do not pull your shoulders up or press backward. Instead, pull up from your hip bones (you'll gain an inch in height if you do this). Hold your shoulders over your hips and align your ears over your shoulders. Now, take deep belly breaths, which will send oxygen through your system.

Here's a good exercise to develop strong breathing: Breathe in and hold your breath for 10 seconds, then release slowly. Gradually increase the seconds you hold and release your breath. You can do this while walking at work or the grocery store or any time you are upright.

Good posture is not just for standing. When you sit, be sure to hold your body in that chair as if you could stand on a second's notice. That means sitting more on the edge of the chair, with your weight off your hip bones. Again, breathe deep belly breaths.

The breathing you'll do while standing or sitting has many benefits. Not only will it help you hold your body correctly, it will lower your heart rate and make you feel less anxious and more in the moment. As a result, you will look more confident (posture) and you will speak more confidently because the breathing will have made your concentration keener.

Gait

Yes, how you walk is part of your appearance, and you are judged on it all the time. Whether you're female or male, it's important to be graceful when you walk. Be light on your feet. Don't clomp around like a horse; walk with dignity and pride, like you take yourself seriously and you care how you look. As you walk, embrace "an innate dignity." Walk with a purpose—like you're in charge of the world.

What to Wear and What Not

One of the biggest mistakes people make with clothing is that they tend to get stuck in the era they felt was their "high-water mark"—the time in their lives in which they felt the most successful and happy and in control. What a mistake that is!

I had a black watch plaid dress that I loved more than anything in 7th grade but I certainly couldn't wear that dress now. I don't think I could even fit my left leg into it! But I have found a very cozy black watch plaid button-down shirt that I wear on days I need to feel a little comfort from a past joyful and carefree time.

What doesn't grow, dies. Remember? Could you imagine a tree holding on to its spring blossoms throughout the summer, autumn, and winter? Flowering trees are so beautiful in April; in November, they'd look a little ridiculous. The same goes for you and your clothes.

"Am I too old to wear this?" "Does this make me look fat?" If you're asking yourself these questions, I think you already know the answers. You need to dress in the way that best flatters not only your age, but also your body type.

It would be impossible for me to address all of these issues with each of you individually, so in the following please find some general guidelines. To understand more specifically how to dress yourself for your age, body type, and profession, I recommend you make an appointment with a personal shopper every three to five years. It's an expense worth incurring because the experience will help you understand how to dress yourself and inform what you buy and how you wear clothes going forward. Sometimes an expense is an investment, and this is a great example of that!

When you shop after your consultation, seek out the advice of salespeople on the floor. You don't have to listen to everything you hear, but if you get a few opinions from people who spend their lives looking at people trying on clothes, you'll go home with purchases that won't be relegated to your closet with the tags still on for the rest of their lives.

▶▶

Words From the Wise—Angelo Lambrou
Clothing Designer/Stylist

Feel Good, Look Good

Dressing up has become much more casual and less interesting. Life has become much more fast-paced. Most people have become less interested in looking special in an outfit that represents themselves and part of the reason is the fashion industry itself. Too much choice, too much information, too many contradictory opinions!

I think that people should take a harsh look at themselves in the mirror (or better yet, see a stylist) every couple of years to assess where they are in life and how their bodies are changing. In a world where everything is made easy for you, individualism has become less important and has led to an inability to decide what works best for you fashion-wise, from your own perspective.

Most people simply rely on trends and what the fashion industry dictates but, unfortunately, what is pushed in your direction as to what you should be wearing will not always suit your style, personality, or body type. More effort needs to be put into identifying what you personally like and dislike for yourself. This will lay the groundwork to making the right decision.

We are all different; we come in all shapes and sizes. By being aware of your body and identifying your best parts, and yes, worst parts, and dressing accordingly, you will put your best foot forward in how you look.

Feeling good in your clothes helps you look better in your clothes, and looking good will create an image of positivity that you project to the world. Looking good can be a life-changing experience. It may land you the chance to meet a date; it may lead to making new friends and will also be helpful in getting that job you've always wanted.

◄◄◄

A Shoe In

It used to be that when I traveled abroad, I could always tell who the Americans were by looking at their shoes. Not so much anymore. We tend to get lured in by the prospect of having lots of pairs of incredibly cheap shoes, when what we should really do is invest in higher-quality classic shoes. Just because shoes are on sale (or are cute) is not a reason to buy them.

If you are not a graceful female, then you need to forget stilettos. If you don't have good balance, then platforms are not for you. You don't have to wear old-lady shoes, but the point of having shoes is to have something you can walk in. If you can't walk in a pair of shoes, then you shouldn't be wearing them.

I'm talking to the men here, too. You may not be as aware of this, but you are also being judged by your shoes! Gentlemen, don't let yourself be swayed by a bargain. Invest in a few pairs of good, expensive shoes and you can't go wrong. And please keep them polished, re-soled, and re-heeled when needed—this goes for men and women. Scuffed shoes are a dead giveaway to sloppiness.

The best time to try on shoes is at the end of the day when your feet are swollen from the day's workout.

And as far as age goes, yes, feet are affected too. As you get older, your feet spread. That's life. If you haven't worn a certain pair of shoes for a few years, it's probably time to get rid of them and replace them with better-quality shoes a half-size larger that you'll actually wear and enjoy. I'm talking here about everyday shoes.

Dress shoes, of course, are a different thing. I'm going to let you in on a little secret: professional dance shoes. They are expensive, yes, often around $300, but they are timeless, beautiful, and made for, well, dancing. Are you the person who takes off your shoes halfway through the wedding? You can keep yourself together for the entire night, without pain, if you wear professional dance shoes. Think about it.

▶▶

Words From the Wise—Alan Matarasso, MD
Board Certified Aesthetic Plastic Surgeon, New York

Saving Face

As we age, we lose volume, so really the trend has been to replace that volume through both fillers and surgery. Cosmetic rejuvenation is done to volumize and treat lines in the face.

Prevention is the best solution—having a good skin care treatment and program, and really treating things as they accrue with age is essential.

Start young in avoiding skin damage. Intervene when necessary. Ninety percent of sun damage occurs before age 22, so young people especially should be wearing sun block daily. Think of the acronym AEM:

Avoidance

Early intervention

Maintenance

In the ideal situation, you take action when you're young—the nonsurgical interventions in order to maintain the skin. When you get to a certain point, you really need to combine both surgical and nonsurgical solutions. Aesthetic surgery will remedy skin looseness and hanging. The nonsurgical cosmetic procedures help soften fine lines, irregular pigment, brown spots, creases, and so forth. In the best of all possible worlds, people would be employing both procedures. You want to start early.

Determining if someone is the right candidate for plastic surgery depends on a host of factors, including a person's history, goals, and an examination. Also, a good plastic surgeon offers alternatives.

There is a lot of talk about the "Liquid Facelift" and that's where many people end up looking ridiculous if they are over-filled in an attempt to "lift up" what's loose. They fill up their face to avoid surgery. They sabotage themselves by going beyond what they should with the fillers, or they do a whole burst of something at once and they don't look right. The correct approach would be to do a small amount of filler, and then maintain the look in order to look natural. And then at a certain point you'll need surgery; fillers alone will not lift sagging skin. It's like saying, should I buy socks or shoes? You need both. They complement and enhance each other. "Lifts lift and fillers fill."

Men have to be especially careful when undergoing aesthetic surgical and nonsurgical procedures to avoid looking overdone. Women have more options and what looks good on a woman will not often look as good on a man. What is common for males and will help give a boost to their appearance as they age are neck lifts and eyelid lifts. Other procedures can make a man's face look too artificial.

Before you undergo cosmetic surgery, be sure your surgeon is matching your disagreeable biological condition with the appropriate treatment. You also need to understand the limitations of cosmetic surgery—the surgeon must work with what's available. Lastly, you want to work with an honest, board-certified plastic surgeon who tells you all of the options available, plus the risks, complications, and alternative treatments. It's important to work with someone who is honest with you.

The whole key is doing work at certain stages in one's life, doing the right amount, and selecting the right surgeon. There are many very good surgeons who can give you an unoperated-on look. The goal is to look better, not different.

The bottom line is to take care of yourself. People get confused and think surgical and nonsurgical aesthetic interventions are interchangeable. They work hand in hand, not necessarily separately.

◀◀◀

Just Face It!

We tend to favor the decade in which we were the happiest not only with wardrobe but with hair and makeup as well. Well, you're not getting any younger and that's okay. If you try to look 20 when you're 50, you're just going to look silly.

Should you get Botox or a facelift? That's up to you. You carry your life in your face as you age. If you think you will feel better smoothing out some of those "rough times," that's what you should do. Just don't overdo it!

One thing people overlook, if you'll pardon the pun, is their eyeglasses. Nothing makes a person look more outdated than an old pair of crummy eyeglasses. Each season there are some quirky trends that you might find appealing as an accent piece. I'm not saying you have to change your eyeglasses four times a year! But maybe when you have an eye exam every couple of years or so, look at the frames available. If your prescription changes, consider a new frame instead of just replacing the lenses of your old frames.

For the guys, be aware of your facial hair. Trends change all the time. Few things will make you look more dated than a mustache style that was popular in another decade and which hasn't become a "retro rage" just yet.

And teeth! So many people don't realize what an impact their teeth make on their appearance and health. A regular teeth cleaning is essential. Scrutinize your smile. Are your teeth crooked, yellow, or gray? All of these potential pitfalls can be easily fixed. Invisible braces not only straighten your teeth but, as a result, improve your self-confidence. Teeth whiteners have come a long way. I'm not suggesting getting veneers that shine like 500-watt light bulbs and can look very artificial. Simple and not terribly expensive procedures are now available to make your teeth sparkle again.

Next are some Words from the Wise tips for men and women from makeup pro Lana Gersman, but keep in mind that these are general tips. Take advantage of the makeup counters found at any department store for a "free" consultation on how your makeup should look. (The word "free" is in quotation marks because though there isn't a charge for these makeup pros to give you a makeover, you are generally expected to buy something.) If you're being made up in front of a mirror, pay attention to the way the makeup pro is using her tools and ask her questions.

This is for men too. Although I'm not advocating you go and slather makeup all over your face, you might get advice on using a moisturizer or doing something to control your eyebrows. People notice scraggly skin and eyebrows and other facial hair that grows like weeds, and as you get older, eyebrows especially will grow out of control. Get some grooming tips and keep it up on your own. You won't regret it!

▶▶▶

Words From the Wise—Lana Gersman
Makeup Artist to the Stars

Putting Your Best Face Forward

I do consultations with people who don't realize they have frozen their face in the decade they were their happiest. It's important to keep updating the way you do makeup as you age. Less is more. It's you who should stand out, *not* your makeup.

Quick Tips for Women

Instead of a face full of foundation, try something like Armani's Fluid Sheer, which comes in many shades. It brightens the skin and gives it a lovely glow.

A heavy concealer might cover dark circles but, without question, it will also bring attention to the lines under your eyes. I prefer to pat in a liquid foundation a shade darker than what we have been traditionally fed. The lighter the concealer, the easier it is to notice dark eye circles coming through. A salmon color for light skins and a matching skin tone for dark is my gauge. Add it to the inner and outer corners of the eyes as well. It's all about brightening your face without it being obvious.

Use base foundation to cover the reddish areas only, often around the corners of the mouth, under the eyes, and inner and outer corners. Spot the foundation and blend. Powder these areas with a sheer invisible powder. Over this, add a medium Bronzer, but not too dark. Focus mostly on the forehead, the nose, the top of the cheekbones, the chin—the areas that the sun would hit. The point is not to mask your face, which too many women do as they get older.

Use a rouge or tinted cheek color as opposed to a powder blush, which often sits on the top of the skin. Start with a little dot the size of a dime on each cheek and blend it by turning the small circle of color into larger circles but making sure it's a flush of color and not a patch.

Always groom your brows, but don't make them harsh or tattoo them. Too many women have what I call "tadpole brows," meaning the front is heavy and the rest is very thin, looking like a tadpole. It should be a high even arch. Add a softer color to them as you get older. Even if you were a brunette, use a pencil or powder color that is several shades lighter.

Women tend to use too thick a mascara that look like spider webs crawling across their face. It looks dirty. Just use mascara on the upper lashes. And if black is too dark, because aging sometimes makes our skin almost sheer, then switch to a brown, focusing on the majority of color at the base of the lashes rather than the length. It's the saturation at the base of the lashes that makes the eye pop. I have seen these horrible spider-like lashes that cling together in the most frightening formations because they are overdone. Again, it's *you* who should stand out, not the makeup.

Blocks of eye shadow should not exist. Just soft sweeps of natural colors are best. Blending is the key.

Long square nails are creepy. Let the nail look like it grew from under the skin and not rise above it. A fingernail should look soft and gently manicured, not like a talon.

For lips, avoid dark colors and always check it's not coloring your teeth. The finger in your mouth and lips curled around it should take excess off as you take it out of your mouth. Soft creamy or sheers, bright (not dark) lip colors are best. Our lips can change shape and look cruel as we get older, so adding a dark color can enhance the negative.

I believe Botox is the greatest discovery. It really softens wrinkles. I have used it since 2002, knowing that my family has a history of deep lines on their foreheads. And when it wears off, it's a softer frown.

Fillers don't work for fine features. "My dermatologist won't let me use any fillers. If I added filler to the lines around my mouth, it would make me look like a chipmunk," clients have said. I see a lot of these creatures walking the streets of Manhattan and Los Angeles.

The point is subtlety. You will never look like you did 30 years ago, just a better version of what you are now.

Quick Tips for Men

Men should moisturize immediately after showering. I see more and more men doing this, but there are still too many who do not. If men (especially bald men) have a very shiny face, they should prep thereafter with an anti-shine in a medium tone.

To cover grays, I see men dying their hair one dark color, which looks so obvious and ridiculous. The hair is made of many colors, however subtle, and so I would suggest going for gentle highlights that blend in with the gray. The use of one flat color brings the eye right to it. You want *you* to stand out, not the flat color of your hair.

If you're balding, should you shave your head? I just worked with Sting who has recently shaved his. He looks great. He realized he is not the man he was 35 years ago. He is now a husband, father, and grandfather. He is aware of the evolution of Sting, from looks to music. You also need to be aware of the evolution of you.

◄◄

You Are What You Eat

My mother never had a weight problem, yet somehow she had overweight kids. It wasn't what she fed us. Part of it had to do with my father's genes and part of it had to do with what we would try to feed ourselves. I still remember my mother saying to me, "You only need to have a taste of it. Don't overdo it!" when it came to desserts and other things that weren't quite the best for us to eat, but were too delicious not to.

It's good advice. You don't have to have three tablespoons of ice cream—have one. Savor the experience and move on. This is how the most successful weight-loss programs work, like Weight Watchers, for example. It's not about depriving yourself completely, it's about prioritizing. Weight Watchers uses a system of points; other systems work other ways. If you're serious about losing weight to feel better in your clothes, see your doctor and/or a nutritionist and get on a program that will work for you.

I'm not going to get too far into this; this is not a book on nutrition and fitness, but your weight is a very important component of your appearance and self-esteem, that's why I'm bringing attention to it. It doesn't mean you need to obsess over it though. I can remember once complaining to my father, a WWII vet, "I have fat legs!" His response to me: "Be grateful; at least you have legs."

▶▶

Words From the Wise—John Foreyt, PhD
Professor, Department of Medicine and Department of Psychiatry and Behavioral Sciences, Baylor College of Medicine

Healthy Weight
You don't have to be skinny to be healthy. The bottom line for all of us is health, not weight. There is a range of weight, not a specific number on the scale, which is healthy for us. We are all different depending on our genes, biochemistry, metabolism, and so on. God made us in all shapes and sizes and the bottom line for all of us is to try to eat healthy and be physically active every day.

The first step in behavior change is always self-awareness. Start by making small changes, one day at a time, every day. It's not easy. If it were easy, everyone would be skinny. But luckily the new obesity guidelines just published point out that a weight loss of just 3 percent has been shown to result in lowered cardiovascular risk, including improvements in blood pressure, lipids, and type 2 diabetes.

People who have lost a lot of weight and kept it off report that they sleep about eight hours a night, eat breakfast, walk, keep a food diary, weigh themselves, and have a support person or group. I'd add they never give up.

For losing weight, reducing blood pressure, lowering blood sugar or bad cholesterol (LDL), it's essential to make dietary changes. A food diary, (which everyone hates keeping because they are boring and monotonous) should be kept for two weeks initially, including writing down the usual, including foods and drinks consumed, and looking up the calories, fat grams, food groups, or points.

After getting a feel for what foods and drinks need changing, the next step is to look for reasons why it's so difficult to change a diet. Usually it's habits or emotions like stress, tension, anxiety, anger, depression, loneliness, and boredom. Those are not easy to change but it is possible. Anything you can identify can be changed, slowly.

We find the best strategy to help change negative moods is walking. We all know physical activity is good for us but, in addition to burning calories, it improves our mood and increases our feeling of well-being making dietary changes easier (it's easier to eat healthy when we feel good than when we feel bad). Again, a little each day works. And more is even better.

◀◀

Work It Out!

Again, this is not a book about fitness and nutrition, but being fit, being healthy, really does wonders for your appearance. Not only does good health show in your body (clothing size, etc.), it also shows in your skin tone. Getting regular exercise and being stronger and fit will make you feel better about yourself, and that will show in your appearance.

My main recommendation is for you to invest in a session or several sessions with a personal trainer. Before you balk at the expense, keep in mind that you don't have to commit to a trainer (or even a gym membership) for life. Like the personal shopper and the makeup consultant, a personal trainer can analyze your goals and show you how to achieve them—without hurting yourself!

▶▶

Words From the Wise—Ricardo Morales
Certified Personal Fitness Trainer at Equinox

Keeping Fit

We always want to help people achieve their fitness goals and make sure the process includes getting them what they need. To figure out what a client needs for a workout, I conduct a fitness assessment with baseline measurements. I assess mobility and stability through a Functional Movement Screen, as well as conduct strength and flexibility assessments. My client's body mechanics let me know if corrective exercises are first needed before we begin to build their strength. In doing this, I'm able to tailor the workout routine and prevent injuries. I go over their weaknesses and imbalances, and try to explain why I've chosen the particular training style and programming approach for them and why they will gain from my chosen routines.

I talk with my clients about their goals and analyze their current routines and activity. Then, when they may lose motivation, I remind them of their original commitment and the reasons they started this journey. This is generally a good time to reassess and review progress, and potentially adjust goals. I keep clients inspired, informing them of their progress and continuing to set attainable goals.

I love what I do and I know results can come if clients stick with the programs I have created specifically for them. I'm very realistic with my clients and I let them know that I understand it's hard, but if they follow a prescribed program, they will see the results. I don't let negativity discourage me, and I maintain my positive and upbeat attitude no matter what.

I advise my clients to:

1. Drink more water.
2. Get more, better sleep.
3. Schedule your workouts like appointments.
4. Alternate strength/cardio/recovery.

◀◀

Bottom Line

Anyone who tells you that your appearance doesn't matter is lying to you. When you invest in your appearance, you're investing in *you*. When you invest in you, it means you know that you are worth something, and when you project that you have worth, the world will see it and believe it too.

6

Image

There is nothing worse than a sharp image of a fuzzy concept.
—Ansel Adams

I had the good fortune of attending a Master Class hosted by four-time Grammy winner and opera superstar, "the People's Diva," Renée Fleming. One of the many wise statements she said to a sold-out house at Carnegie Hall was in response to a question by a young singer. The woman asked what advice Ms. Fleming would give to those who are starting out in the world of opera. Renée without hesitation said, "Protect your image on social media."

She went on to say that she vigilantly works at managing what is released about her, her life, and her career. She added that if one bad picture or unfortunate quote gets released into the great ether, you run the risk of it going viral.

You're not an opera diva, but the same social media lesson applies to you, no matter what industry you're working in or want to work in.

We just looked at how you look—your physical appearance. But in this day and age, you will likely never come face-to-face with so many people you need to impress. They will get to know you from your correspondence, your e-mails, and your social media presence. It won't matter in these instances whether or not you've had your teeth whitened. What will matter is that, in the one-dimensional world of an end-user's interface with a computer screen or magazine, you come across as an interesting, intriguing, and multi-dimensional person.

Easy enough, right? Ha! (Don't panic.)

To present yourself in the most effective fashion, you first need to know yourself, inside and out. In this chapter, I'll help you get to the core of who you are and understand how to present that person to the world beyond the screen.

In this chapter, you'll also see how not knowing who you are wastes your time and others' and sabotages your ability to connect with them. You'll discover how social media has changed the way you present yourself. And you'll learn how to present yourself multi-dimensionally in a one-dimensional world.

It's All About Me!

Yes. Yes it is! But also, it isn't.

Though it may have seemed somewhat surprising in 2006 that *Time* magazine's Person of the Year was "You," now it's commonplace. Social media has cracked open the world, and *you* are now the most influential person in your world today. We live in an intensely "me-centric" world, increasingly "me-centric" actually, thanks to social media.

If you're of the older generations, you may be cringing right now at just the words "social media." Well, get over yourself. In the past decade, the world and your place in it has been changing rapidly. Consider that at the start of the 21st century, there really wasn't any social media at all. Then:

- ▶ LinkedIn reached out at the end of 2002 and formally launched in 2003.
- ▶ Facebook showed its face on the scene in February of 2004.
- ▶ Twitter "hatched" on July 15, 2006.
- ▶ YouTube debuted in February of 2005 but really exploded when Google took it over in 2006.
- ▶ Instagram popped up in 2010 but really took off in 2012 and hasn't shown any sign of stopping.
- ▶ Google+ added itself to the ring on June 28, 2011.
- ▶ Pinterest got started in September 2011 and really stuck.

Then...well, heaven knows what's being cooked up right now in college dorms. The point is, social media made a splash this past decade and it shows no signs of drying up any time soon.

It's also not just "for kids." I have had many older clients tell me that social media was not for them—that they felt, at their age, they were above it, that it was silly somehow to put yourself out there on social media. Think of it this way: in this world, if someone wants to know more about you, you are just a Google search away. Shouldn't you want to have some control over what comes up when you get Googled?

Older readers take note: according to a 2013 study, Twitter usage for people ages 55–64 had grown exponentially since 2012—a 79 percent increase! For Facebook, it has been a 46 percent increase, for Google+, 56 percent.

So if you think social media is not for you, you're wrong. It has a ton to do with you and with all of us. Younger users already know the value and impact of social media. The next generation won't even have an experience of the world without it!

I want you to really think about how different the ways that you can express yourself have become over the past 10 years—whether you're 25 or 40 or 65. The world has become, and becomes more so, "about you."

Consequently, if you have the world right where you want it, why aren't you fully capitalizing on the power of you and reaping all the benefits? Why aren't you looking the best you can out there in this "you" landscape?

This actually has to do with a concept that predates all of this social media madness: personal brand.

Brand New You?

The idea of personal brand seems old and crusty by now, but it's still relevant. And it's evolving all the time. As important as it is for people to quickly understand and express themselves as their own personal brand, when I challenge participants to tell me in just a few words just who they are, 99 percent of the time I'm faced with blank stares.

The trouble is that many of us just don't know who we are. Sure, we have an inkling, and we try to fake it where we can. But that's just not an option anymore. Only when you understand and present the real you to the world, will you be able to advance. It's high time you figured that out.

The idea of working with SPARC buddies will carry through in nearly everything you do in this book, especially in this chapter. Having someone to bounce off your idea about your image with is invaluable because it's almost impossible to see oneself objectively.

Let's look at SPARC as it has to do with image.

- ▶ Strategy: What are you trying to achieve with your image?
- ▶ Purpose: Why is presenting yourself in the best light possible important to accomplishing your strategy?
- ▶ Analyze: Which elements of your current image are working for you? Which are not?
- ▶ Rehearse: How will you focus your efforts to developing your image?
- ▶ Commit: How will you make your image impactful and indelible?

These threads will be woven in throughout this chapter, challenging you to really think through all the decisions you make. Collaborate with a SPARC buddy to ensure you are following the plan.

So Who the Heck Are You?

If you don't know who you are, there's no way you're going to be able to go out there and sell yourself to others. Have you ever tried to sell anything, such as a glass of lemonade to neighborhood passersby when you were a kid? Or a new TV when you worked at the electronics store while you put yourself through college? Or a new creative package to a client who may not be sure he or she even wants a new creative package? You knew in all of these situations that the way you were going to sell these things was to understand exactly and succinctly what you were selling, and to make it appealing to your buyer.

It's totally the same when it comes to selling *you*—in person or on screen. It all comes down to knowing exactly who you are. Only then can you properly present yourself.

What's Your Point?

I have an exercise I do in seminars that really helps clients quickly and easily get to the nut of who they are. It's something that's really easy for anyone to grasp—anyone who has had more than a first-grade-level education. I call it "Personal Punc-h."

I ask: If you were a punctuation mark, what would you be? It seems like an odd question, especially odd in a board room or auditorium packed with C-Suite executives for sure. But in my experience, I have seen that it's actually the simplest way for people to encapsulate themselves and explain who they are to others.

Take me, for example. My corporate logo is a trademarked bright red "!". It was inspired by my book, *Get to the Point!*, but through the years has resonated as a symbol of my message that people immediately get.

Recently, as I tried to come up with an easy way for people to start understanding their personality type, I happened to glance down at my logo and it just hit me: I am a quintessential exclamation point. I am optimistic and energetic; I am aggressive and sometimes a little over the top. But whatever emotions the mark conjures, I am easily and comfortably defined by it.

That led me to think of other punctuation marks, and to see my friends, family members, and clients as punctuation. I started asking people and they immediately got it:

- ► "I'm a colon because I always have more to say."
- ► "I'm a semicolon because I am a connector of ideas."
- ► "I'm a question mark because I always want to know more."
- ► "I'm a period because I like closure and demand it from others."
- ► "I'm a comma, with semicolon rising...a work in progress."

Take a quick look at the following chart to see the basic characteristics attributable to each mark and which best describes your Personal Punc-h.

Your Personal Punc-h

Mark	What Does It Mean?	What to Celebrate	What to Work On
!	Energetic, innovative, assertive, ambitious, enthusiastic, self-reliant, confident, determined.	Your boundless energy, your passion.	Your quick temper, seeming too aggressive, cocky, or stubborn.
?	Speculative, ambitious, curious, thoughtful, imaginative, resourceful.	Your unparalleled research and investigative skills, your boundless desire to want to know more.	Stopping yourself from actually "doing" because you're too busy thinking. Seeming much too nosy.
.	Practical, responsible, sensible, logical, analytical, highly discriminating.	Your careful planning, your precise, scientific approach to life.	Being inflexible, not being open to ideas that may be different than yours, stubbornness.
;	Philosophical, intellectual, studious, farseeing.	Your flexibility and versatility. Your ability to see more than one side in any situation.	Being restless and sometimes too indecisive.
:	Methodical, businesslike, organizational, multitasking.	Your impeccable management skills, your ability to keep many thoughts in line at once.	Taking on too much and overwhelming others.
,	Team player, diplomat, clarifier, peacemaker.	Your ability to help others make sense, your sense of compassion, always helping the cause along.	Being too wishy-washy, sacrificing your own best interests for the good of the group, shyness.

Though every mark is important, a comma can be absolutely crucial to ensuring success. As Lynne Truss proved with her hilarious book on punctuation, *Eats, Shoots and Leaves*, one misplaced comma translates to a panda bear with a smoking gun.

One Word Is Worth a Thousand Pictures

When someone asks you to describe yourself, can you summarize who you are in a paragraph or in a sentence? Most people struggle with this. For that reason, I generally ask people to list those words—they could be nouns, verbs, or adjectives—that best describe them.

Most people don't take into consideration who their audience is. You may be some version of yourself during a PTA meeting and another version of yourself at a business networking meeting and another version of yourself at a customer meeting, but there will be facets of you that blend into all aspects of your life.

When you craft your "about you" paragraph, you're going to want to leave room for about 10 words that hit the target audience in the gut, the example of what you can do for "those" issues, "that" project, "their" charity event. So in a 40-word, 15-second elevator pitch, 65 percent of that pitch can be used across all audiences, leaving 35 percent for customization.

Who Are You?

Take out your journal and open it to a fresh page. Now take a few minutes to think about words that work to describe you and list 10 of them on the page.

Next, step back and take a look at that list. What do you see? Are most of the words one part of speech—more nouns than verbs or more adjectives than nouns? If so, which of these parts of speech is dominating?

Read off the words one by one. How do they sound when spoken out loud? How do they resonate with your SPARC buddy? Do any sound artificial and forced when they come out of your mouth? Do any really satisfy? Your SPARC buddy will be of enormous help to you in this case. It's excruciatingly difficult for any of us to write adequately about ourselves for so many reasons. But more than ever we must write about ourselves daily, whether it's simply e-mail in our company or being active with social media. And, once it's out there, it's there forever.

If any of your listed words sound forced when you speak them, you need new words. Go back to the list and keep trying out new words until they all feel right.

Making "You" Work

Once you have your list of 10 words, it's time to create a short paragraph about you. Let's say your list included words such as:

1. Enthusiastic.
2. Self-starter.
3. Team player.
4. Resourceful.
5. Well-connected.
6. Detail oriented.
7. Facile (effortless) thinker.
8. Proficient writer.
9. Articulate.
10. Innovator.

The next step would be to put an interrogation lamp on those words:

▶ Enthusiastic—Big deal. Give an example why that's important. Are you undaunted when obstacles fall in your path? Do you lead people through firestorms? When did this happen and what does it mean to your audience?

▶ Self-starter—Excellent attribute. How did that help your organization? You're a manager's dream candidate or nightmare depending on how controlling your manager is.

▶ Team player—Everyone says that, but can you be a team player who isn't afraid of saying what everyone else is thinking, in such a way that doesn't offend?

▶ Resourceful—Oh sure, we all say that. But if you metaphorically pulled a rabbit out of a hat, tell us how.

▶ Well-connected—Always a desirable trait as long as you have a track record. Give specifics.

► Detail oriented—Maybe a fine a characteristic, but perhaps you get buried in the weeds. Again, provide an example of how this attribute helped in a real situation.

► Facile thinker—Really? Prove it. How did you pull the proverbial body from the wreckage with your quick thinking?

► Proficient writer—Your boss leans on you for research? You've published papers? Examples are needed.

► Articulate—If you are to be a spokesperson for the team, or want to be, then your elevator pitch needs to be inspirational in tone.

► Innovator—Wonderful. What have you designed or created? If ever there were a time in our history where innovators are applauded, it is now.

In your 40-word paragraph, you must give an example of how these attributes will help the audience to whom you are speaking or writing: 65 percent should be from your template and 35 percent customized for your specific audience. You'll use this paragraph to become the base for your elevator pitch—40 words spoken in 15 seconds that hit the nail on the head about you. We'll get more into this in the next chapter.

Crafting Your Paragraph

Now that you have interrogated yourself, possibly, hopefully, with your SPARC buddy, it's time to put this in paragraph form.

1. Get rid of unimportant words such as, "My name is...." Just say your name and cite your specialty. In my case, I would say: "Karen E. Berg, Communication Coach. Message Development and Delivery."

   I don't say, "I specialize in" or "my experience is" because these are useless words. This is where the Twitter 140-character model is especially helpful. Every character counts. Monitor your word choices and make every word count.

2. Identify your audience. Then you're into what all those descriptive words can do for that audience, for that project, for that team, for that fundraiser. Sell yourself!

You're now saying: "But, I'm not a salesperson." Today, with social media and with employment, or lack thereof, we are all salespeople, 24/7. But we're subtle in our sales; we're not hammering people over their heads. We're engaging them.

3.   Time your elevator pitch. Listen to your voice (more on voice in Chapter 7). You want to strive for 15 seconds, but don't talk fast just to make that time allocation. If you know newspaper editors, or maybe you are one, you know the anguish of having to delete what you might consider stunning prose. Less is *always* more in social media. We all have the attention span of a gnat nowadays. Is it a good trait? Nope, but it's reality.

4.   Revise, edit, rehearse, and re-record. Time it. I think you'll be great.

5.   Go out and *win*.

▶▶

Words From the Wise—Scott Warren
Life Style Designer

Finding "You" In Words

The best 10 words that describe what I do would be as follows:

Listen	Solve
Innovate	Mediate
Focus	Simplify
Create	Integrate
Define	Polish

Words like "beautiful," "elegant," or "high-end" may sound more appropriate when thinking of a designer. However, I have found that, almost in order, the previous list pretty much sums up a regular project with a normal client.

◀◀

Getting to Know Yourself

Here's another quick way to get to know more about yourself. Open your journal and write your answers out as sentences (for example, "When I was growing up, I wanted to be Neil Armstrong"), then reflect on what you see:

- ▶ When you were growing up, who did you want to be?
- ▶ If a movie were to be made about your life, what would it be called and who would play you?
- ▶ Are you religious, spiritual, or materialistic?
- ▶ What truly motivates you? If it helps you, the mantra I live by is: time is money. Whatever I do, I have to get paid. There has to be some incentive, though that doesn't necessarily mean cash. If it doesn't feed my bank account then it must feed my soul.
- ▶ Aside from work, name five things that interest you.
- ▶ Aside from work, name five things that might interest you about others.
- ▶ What are your top five books?
- ▶ What are your five favorite movies?
- ▶ What's your favorite color?
- ▶ What's your favorite season?

Are there any themes running through these answers? For example, do you like action movies and/or spy novels? Does lighter fare light up your life? For instance, does comedy and romance factor in here? Are you more concerned with yourself or others? What drives you?

Your Image on Paper

When I give a seminar, I typically take examples of people's business cards, company brochures, and other printed collateral, and demonstrate what works, what ties into the brand these items are supposed to represent, and what does not.

Most people have no idea about all of the elements they should include in their arsenal to reinforce their brand identity.

Look, as much as you want to believe it is so, paper isn't dead in this digital world. You will always need a nice business card. Depending on your industry, printed post cards, brochures people can hold in their hands, and portfolios to actually thumb through with an actual thumb, can all be essential to your image.

Here's something most people never consider in this day and age: having nice stationery. A handwritten note gets noticed. It's a good idea to hone your cursive and start sending folks handwritten notes on nice paper that reflects who you are and what you do. Have you noticed that in our digital age, our handwriting has become unintelligible? Or is it just me? The texture, the color, the imagery—all of these matter in your printed materials. Think before you print!

▶▶

Words From the Wise—Scott Warren
Life Style Designer

The Impact of Color

Color is something that I find affects most aspects of our lives. We all identify with a favorite; we all have one we hate. It affects us on obvious levels, like when an advertiser uses green to connote "fresh" or a red to say "spicy" or "fast" (think about car commercials using red cars).

But there are also many subconscious uses of color we never notice. Would you feel comfortable if your surgeon or dentist wore bright red scrubs? I bet not, which is why they are always a soothing shade of green or blue. Why are men's prisons beginning to use pink as their favorite paint and apparel choice? It's because it has shown to create a much more docile population by increasing estrogen production and calming testosterone-flush inmates. Why are all the fast food logos red and yellow? Think of In-N-Out Burger; they want us to be interested to stop and feel hungry (red) and in a hurry to move on and get going (yellow).

As for the color association to punctuation I see things this way:

▶ Exclamation points are undoubtedly *red*. They're practically shouting at you. Red is high energy, bold, stimulating, invigorating, menacing, demonstrative, and fierce.

▶ Question marks are blue—open-ended, like the depths of the ocean or the distant sky.

▶ Periods are taupe, earth color. They are final, grounded, and expected.

▶ Colons are black, tailored, and sleek, serving an exact purpose while adding structure and definition.

▶ Semicolons are white because there is a blank slate ahead wanting to be completed.

▶ Commas make me think "green" because after a comma something new must always follow. Think fresh, forward, next, and more.

◀◀

The Man (or Woman) Behind the Screen

There's no business like show business—and all business is "show."

To an extent, this is true and definitely so on social media. Forget about the old "15 minutes of fame" here, though, because 15 minutes is an eternity in social media terms. Depending on how many others are reading your statuses and tweets, viewing your videos and Vimeos, sampling your pictures and your Pinterest, you're lucky to grab 15 seconds.

Social media is incredibly visual, so before you open your mouth to speak, so to speak, on social media, you better make sure your image conveys what you want people to know about you in a flash.

▶▶

Words From the Wise—Jeff Winton
Senior Vice President/Chief Communications Officer
at Astellas Pharma

Communication Changes—For Better or Worse?

During the past five years, communications has changed dramatically, as we are now living in a 24/7 news cycle. In the early 1980s, you literally had an entire day to fix something that may have occurred before the next day's paper was printed. We don't have that luxury now. Any mistake or erroneous information travels like wildfire, and it can be virtually impossible to fix.

We are now using social media in the same way we once used telexes and faxes. Instead of calling a reporter or solely sending out a press release, we are now tweeting our news to these same target audiences, and responding to queries via e-mail rather than returning phone calls.

Because of this and the necessity of having staff members who understand technology and new tools like Twitter, we are now hiring "digital natives," 23-year-olds right out of college, as people of my generation continue to struggle to keep up with the rapidly evolving world. But I believe that members of my generation need to try their best to keep up with the new technology and platforms, and not let the world pass us by. I think it's important to at least be conversant about the new landscape and be willing to embrace it and keep pace with the changes.

◀◀

Your Home Base

It doesn't really matter what industry you're in, in this day and age, you should have a Web presence. Even if you have presence all across the social media landscape, it's important to have a place to come home to.

What you'll feature as your Web presence will depend on what kind of profession you're in. If you're a journalist, you'll have your articles or links to articles. A graphic designer might create an online portfolio. An attorney's Website might be as basic as a home page with an interesting biography, photo, and contact information.

What is the easiest way to know what should go there? Google your profession and the word "Website," and look at the sites of the top hits. Examine what colleagues and competitors are doing/have done. Take notes on what you like and don't like about the Web presences of others, and develop your content around that.

You can hire someone to create your Web presence, though there are many programs available now featuring thousands of templates, some free and some that you may need to pay a small fee to use, that can help you create your own.

▶▶▶

Words From the Wise—Jeremy Merrifield
Creative Director/Cofounder Jupiter Highway

Mind Your (Online) Business

One of the biggest mistakes businesses make for their Websites, and for their entire visual program, is that they don't budget enough for marketing. People think that marketing is something to "add on" to an existing business when, in fact, it *is* your business plan. You can have a great product, but if your marketing isn't amazing, no one will know about it. Instead, have a good product, launch with amazing marketing, and use the sales to iterate that good product into a great product. One of the best examples of this is Apple's iPhone and its brilliant marketing and product evolution.

People also tend to think they're smarter at marketing now because they can turn to social media, but social media is only as good as the strategy that's been applied to it. In fact, social media shouldn't be considered an advertising channel at all. It's a content stream created to offer value to your consumer base, with an occasional bit of self-promotion.

Many businesses say they don't have time for social media or think just buying an ad is enough to say they're "marketing." Customized content, meaning video and imagery, for your customer relationships is more important than ever, and social networks allow you to scale those relationships and keep the conversation fresh and tailored to your consumers. Putting money into your local newspaper ad would be better spent developing custom content that would excite your existing consumer base and draw new consumers to you. You either need to make the time to devote to this, or you need to hire someone and work with them so they understand your business goals.

Also, businesses need to leverage technology. There's a thriving digital community out there filled with your customers, potential customers, and competitors—your presence there is crucial.

If a customer can't find you on Google Maps, peruse your services/products on their phone maps, peruse your services/products in your app, or tweet to you, you might as well not exist at all.

◄◄

LinkedIn for Hooking Up?

Social media is a series of parties, all happening at once.

Think of Facebook's dynamic to be like a family reunion in which you know, or sort of know, everyone and you're connected by sharing experiences, many of them common. Communication happens informally at the group level; conversations spark in the comments threads.

Twitter is like a large, mostly anonymous cocktail party. You enter the room (feed), you twitter about, reading what's trending, listening to the conversations of others. You break in quickly and succinctly, make your introduction (in 140 characters or less), there may or may not be interaction, and you quickly move on.

Thinking in those terms, LinkedIn, then, is like a professional conference. You exchange business cards (connect) and don't interact quite as much, saving the information you've collected to reach out later.

Because LinkedIn is a professional site, it's where you need to promote your professional self. You should have a photo in place on your profile, and it should not be a photo of you at a backyard barbecue or in informal wear.

It should not be a photo of you with your spouse or kids or dog or anyone. It should not be a cutesy cartoon avatar.

You should interact often with LinkedIn because it is a proven fact that business comes from here. I learned that a few years ago when a client with whom I had had no contact with for nearly 10 years found me on LinkedIn. I metaphorically kiss that platform everyday because of its networking potential.

Keep your resume up to date. Your credentials should be impressive and succinct. You should try and collect endorsements from people who have worked with you and can recommend you at length—not the ones that say "Johnny endorsed you for...marketing" or "Mary endorsed you for...bookkeeping." Rather, get statements that are several sentences long by people who have worked with you and want to recommend you to others. To get these, you may have to do some endorsement yourself, but be discerning. Don't just recommend anyone. Like anything else in social media, once it's out there, you can never take it back.

The people in my life are very engaged in discussion groups. I suggest that people start a group, lead, and manage it; become a thought leader of a specific topic or issue.

▶▶▶

Words From the Wise—Chuck Pineda, PE/CGC/AVS
President/Managing Director, Trans-Infra PPP, LLC

Discussion Groups

Given the current environment, which includes many Web-based social and professional networking sites, I have found that it's almost de rigueur to be "plugged into" this resource pool of information. As a professional in the architectural and engineering consulting business serving potential clients across the U.S., Canada, and abroad, it became apparent several years ago that an excellent and cost-effective way to connect to people and join the global conversation was by utilizing select networking site(s) that accommodated specific discussion groups, allowing sharing of information on specific topics and bringing together academics, professionals, and knowledgeable people in that field.

I regularly participate in various discussion groups on the Web, some of which I have joined and some that I initiated. Participation in these groups has been extremely beneficial for many reasons, including professional growth and development as well as identifying potential clients, professional resources/talent, and work opportunities.

Many highly capable people are eager to share their experiences with others. By doing so, they not only help to more efficiently progress general knowledge and prevent others from making the same costly mistakes, but they assist the development of young professionals as well.

Identifying the experts and knowledgeable people within a particular field or industry is one of the most useful aspects of the discussion groups. Headhunters and industry recruiters openly admit that they now use the Internet exclusively for identifying talent and regularly look into specific discussion groups to find talent in a particular area.

◀◀◀

There's Egg on Your Face(book)

What is Facebook for? To look at what some people post up there, you would think self-promotion, self-promotion, self-promotion, and also, self-promotion. Then there are others who post anything and everything, from questionable photographs (more common with younger users) to appalling detail about physical maladies, too much information about marital strife and other relationship issues, and gripes about work. Guess what, folks? Even if you're not friends with your boss on Facebook, he or she might still be able to see what you post. Even if you're meticulous about your privacy settings (and most of you are not), there are back doors everywhere for people to sneak through and spy on you.

Be careful.

I'm going to admit something to you. The first thing I do when I'm hired as a coach is I go and check out that person on Facebook. Many people have very loose privacy settings and there's lots I can see, even if I'm not a "friend" of that person. If I'm a "friend" of a "friend" of that person,

I can sometimes see more. I get a background on that person, and I judge what kind of person he or she is by what she or he has posted. And I look at your YouTube videos as well. Is it fair? Absolutely not, but it's a reality of our digital life.

Imagine all the potential clients, employers, casting directors, and admissions agents who are actively on Facebook and doing the same.

Before you slap anything onto your Facebook, take five minutes away from it. At the end of five minutes, things that seemed impulsively interesting do sometimes (or even most of the time) seem less so. So although you can't technically be fired over something you post on Facebook, you can always be fired for another reason that's given, aside from posts like "My boss is a troll," or "Work is so boring, I could die."

▶▶▶

Words From the Wise—John Frazier
EVP at Quinn Lifestyle Public Relations Agency

Social Media as a Business Tool

Social media has changed so much about communication. It seems people often revert to some digital platform or another rather than speak to each other. I've actually seen people at work tweeting at each other when they were within 10 feet of each other! Is that healthy?

Facebook, I thought, was for college kids, which I guess it originally was. Once I gave in, I was very glad I did because it has become an amazing channel for communicating with so many corners of my life. At Quinn, we have a popular Facebook page with more than 15,000 fans.

We also have a very active Twitter handle for the agency, as we've found that it is an excellent channel for communicating with journalists. Journalists and editors don't seem to answer the phone anymore or even listen to their voicemails, and sometimes Twitter can get you through.

I was an early adopter of Twitter. I had to nudge a lot of people at our PR firm into using Twitter because I thought it was going to be important for our industry. I was right about that, but now I feel like I created a bit of a monster if our people are tweeting each other rather than talking to each other. I've kind of backed off Twitter, though I do find it extremely helpful as a research tool.

As of today, @QuinnPR has 5,599 followers and a huge number of them are the writers and editors we constantly seek to engage. We very often pitch the media via Twitter, and often find the best leads by monitoring the Twitter feeds of the top media we are following. We even once saved a honeymoon from total doom. We saw someone tweet that they'd just checked into our client's hotel for their honeymoon and their room was not as promised. We contacted the resort immediately and voila! Problem fixed equals happy couple!

I personally feel liberated by technology. Though I may now be working just about any time of day or night via my iPhone, it and other means of connection and communication allow me to walk out the door at 5 p.m. on most days. In an odd way, I feel like I have a better work/life balance than ever before.

◀◀◀

Don't Be a "Twit"

As with Facebook, Twitter is not intended as a platform for narcissism and yet it has become one. Scan through your newsfeed and what do you see? Buy me! Read me! Look at me! Love *me*!

What was intended as a forum for active, international engagement sometimes reads like a wall of advertising posters. Don't be one of those posters. You will find yourself not only ignored but unfollowed as well.

This is not to say you shouldn't market yourself, your product, or your services on Twitter, because it's an excellent forum for reaching your customer. You just have to be smart about how you do it.

Remember this formula: 20 percent promotion, 80 percent engagement. For every five tweets you post, only one should be selling. The others should provide a link to an informative article you enjoyed, useful information, or even to engage another Twitter user: "Thanks @bergonpoint, for your book #smartread" or "Love that @panerabread roast beef sandwich #bestfood."

Don't go nuts with the hashtag (#); too many make your posts look like spam. Decide on one or two strategic hashtags per tweet and move on.

If your Twitter account is a mess, it's easier to fix than your Facebook account. On the plus side, depending on how many people follow you, your tweets are there and gone within seconds, minutes, or hours. Unless someone is specifically on your profile reading through all your thousands of tweets, they get buried fast. Also, if you take down a tweet before someone else has engaged with it (retweeted it, favorited it, replied to it) you can make it disappear. Though someone else is not going to take the time to scan through your tweets, you should make that time and make sure everything that's there is something the whole world can see.

Your Twitter profile should feature a photo of you. People tend not to follow profiles that aren't yet "hatched." Your description should be short and succinct. (Remember your elevator pitch.) You should also include your Website in your description. Again, we'll get more into this in the next chapter.

▶▶▶

Words From the Wise—Andre Mechaly
Marketing/Strategy Director—
Network & Infrastructure Systems at Thales

Social Media Matters

I love live tweeting in conferences. This is the best way to get in touch with people who usually are interested in the same topics as you. Live tweeting has allowed me to get in touch with a lot of journalists with whom I would have had many difficulties to get in touch with. And the beauty is that when the journalist reads your tweets, and likes them, you can have very good discussions afterward. It also allowed me to get in touch with a couple of ministers (that I unfortunately didn't meet afterward) and MPs (that I met!).

When somebody looks at your tweets and retweets you, he will usually Google you before deciding to follow you. You need to ensure that your LinkedIn profile is up to date, that it refers to posts you want people to see associated with you, and that your Facebook profile shows things that you want associated with you. When you get a new follower on Twitter this way, it is usually a strong relation so worth the effort!

◄◄

Insta-Fame/Insta-Failure

An instant of fun can lead to a lifetime of liability. The fun about Instagram is the impulsive aspect of it. Take a selfie! Any time! Anywhere! Post it immediately for the entire world to see! Before you post that moment, ask yourself if that's really something that needs to live in perpetuity. Take the five-minute rule you do for Facebook. If it's still interesting five minutes after the fact, it may be okay to post. Just make sure the photo is in good taste and is something you wouldn't mind your boss or your parents seeing.

YouTube Equals the New "Boob Tube"

YouTube gets used for a lot of things these days, but, like all of these areas, I urge you to use it wisely. Many unfortunate things end up on YouTube—many humorous things. But you should be using it as a place to market your brand.

It's become more common than ever now to use video to promote yourself. As a public speaker, it's a medium I've been familiar with for years. But you don't have to be a speaker to have a video of yourself speaking.

▶▶

Words From the Wise—Douglas DeMarco
Executive Producer/Owner Brown Paper Bag, Inc.

The Five Mistakes People Make About Headshots
1. **Over Retouching.** The headshot must look like you, not an idealized version of you. Because retouching is so easy with digital photos (Change your eye color? Make your neck longer? No problem!) people often go overboard. The rule of thumb is that retouching should involve no more than a makeup person could have done when the photos were taken. This leads to...

2. **Their clothes don't fit**. A workshop I took on portraiture showed "before" and "after" photos in which the only retouching was done on the subject's clothes. The results were amazing. Fixing wrinkles, creases, fabric "pops," crooked lapels, and so forth did more for the shot than you could imagine. Your clothes should always be what you feel you look best in (appropriate to the needs of the photo), but they have to fit well.

3. **It's not the DMV!** A headshot should never be taken straight on, and a good photographer will know how to pose you. One trick that works well for men and women is to lean in toward the camera; put your weight on the leg closest to the camera and lean in. The photo will look dynamic, engaging, and natural.

4. **They don't audition the photographer.** Many people will go to a photographer on a friend's recommendation and never look at the work. Go to the photographer's gallery and see what the work is like. Remember, he's putting what he considers his best work online. If all the photos feature outdoor or "natural" photos, you may not get a great "studio" shot.

5. **They pick a photo from the first "roll."** It takes a non-professional (not a model) time to get comfortable in front of a camera. When I shoot headshots, I consider the first hundred photos as "warm-up garbage" and won't even show them to the client. Every shot a client selects as a "potential" or "keeper" comes from the last hundred or so. By then they are warmed up, comfortable with the lights and clicks, and have had time to establish a relationship with the photographer.

◀◀◀

Fools on Film

Always remember: There's no business like show business but *all* business is show!

One of my most successful programs is Communicating The Message: How To Be Camera Ready Anytime Anywhere. In it, I teach that corporations can learn a lot from creative people when it comes to being filmed. We can take a page out of the entertainment industry playbook to really learn how to present ourselves on video. For instance, I know a Tony Award–winning actor who never goes to an audition without being dressed and in makeup for video. She doesn't know if they will be recording her, but she's always ready. The same should be true for you.

Even I have had instances in which I haven't been prepared for video and have been caught in an unflattering moment. For an interview I did about my singing group, I was sitting with the interviewer waiting for the camera to roll. Well, there was no point that the camera began rolling—the filming had begun before the interviewing started. The camera was rolling and I never knew it. Pay attention to the first few seconds of this video clip which you can access through this Web link: *www.youtube.com/watch?v=DVvdDoWAMK0*.

Yes, that's me, media expert, swiping at my nose as the first image anyone will see of me in an otherwise successful five-minute piece.

You need to be ready at all times because you can't assume the person filming you is going to be doing any editing. You need to be "on" before you know the camera is on. You need to be aware of your face, your body, and your actions. See yourself outside yourself.

Let my rubbing my nose waiting for the roll of the camera be a cautionary tale for you. I have been a spokesperson for 30 years. The standards have changed.

Your Video Arsenal

You don't have to invest a lot of money to have a professional platform for video making. You really only need:

▶ A backdrop of blue, green, or soft white. You want the background to be plain, not distracting. You can pick up a fold-up screen that you can easily store when not using for about 70 dollars.

▶ If you prefer a background representing your profession, say a physician's lab or a professor's library, make sure the background enhances rather than distracts. You don't want the viewers' eyes trying to read the titles on the books on your shelves. You want them focused on you!

▶ A tripod, available for a video camera or even a smart phone. You can pick up a sturdy tripod for less than 50 dollars; for an iPhone, a tripod can run around 30 dollars, but there are some cute models you can get for as little as five bucks.

► And don't forget about lighting. If you don't consider yourself savvy about lighting, there are tutorials on YouTube. What you don't want is to end up with "raccoon eyes," that dark shading around your eyes. You want your content to "pop" off the screen rather than the green hue of your skin under poor lighting.

Getting Set Up

Making a good video is not as simple as whipping out your iPhone and recording. Even with a good script and a focused message, there's much preparation you need to do before you even think about turning on that camera.

First, make sure your appearance is the best it can be. Get your hair done. Get your roots touched up. Make sure your teeth are clean. Go get a free "makeover" at the makeup counter of a department store, or pay to have one professionally done.

Next, do you wear eyeglasses? Make sure they're not outdated. Along with a bad hairstyle and bad makeup, nothing makes you look older than wearing outdated eyewear.

Now, what are you wearing? Answer: Not black. Black absorbs the light. Not busy patterns. Small patterns are terrible and can "buzz" on camera; they distract viewers from focusing on you. Women, jewel tone blouses and jackets are lovely on camera. Men, whatever your profession, you can't go wrong in a light-blue or other pastel collared shirt. (Choose your wardrobe to contrast with your background color so you will pop.) Depending on your subject matter and profession, you don't necessarily need to wear a tie, but be neat with clothes pressed.

Lastly, test different angles and distances in the camera. This is a case of don't "lean in" on the camera on the computer. I once attended a video conference call given by the CEO of a large corporation. His face was so close to the screen that it was like watching a giant tuna in an aquarium, eyes bulging out and everything. No one could keep focused on what he was saying because he was so, well, "in your face." Don't let that happen to you! You want to make sure that only your warmth and intelligence comes through.

Grab, Hit, Heal

People sabotage themselves in videos because they don't grab their audience in the first few seconds. And then they ramble on without focus for minutes at a time. They distract the viewer by pacing back and forth, have vocal and/or physical tics, and don't have a clear message. A successful video of you is going to be around 60 seconds and not longer than 90 seconds. Anything more will bore the pants off your audience and completely dilute what you're trying to say.

How can you ensure your video will be a success? Start with knowing your audience. Then tailor a script to speak to that audience. Write out what you want to say and memorize it. Break out the message into five parts.

First, startle and grab. Say you're a graphic designer looking for new Website clients. Start off your video with information that will get their attention, like a startling statistic or a provocative statement like "Did you know you're losing 90 percent of your business?" or "If your Website is more than two years old, it could be a liability for you."

Next, you should convey "I can help; here's how." Again, be sure you tailor your message to your audience with a statement like "For the past five years, I've helped businesses like yours improve sales by helping drive traffic to strategically planned Websites."

Then, visual and voiceover. Create a slide show that shows what you can do. Explain to the viewer what they are seeing and share information to help them absorb the images.

Now, offer a plan to fix and heal. Tell them what you're going to do to help optimize their success. Lay it out for them.

Finally, reinforce and repeat. Remind people in one sentence or less why they need you. Tell them how to find you (reinforced by captions at the bottom of the screen).

Craft a script to cover these bases and you'll be on your way to creating a successful video.

In all of this, don't forget to reach out to your SPARC buddy. From the first draft of your script to the final cut of your video, listen to what they have to say and take their critiques seriously. You may not like everything they're saying, but if you trust that their main objective is to help you improve (and you should, or you need a new buddy), you should follow their advice and make your piece the best it can be.

▶▶▶

Words From the Wise—Jeremy Merrifield
Creative Director/Cofounder Jupiter Highway

Using Social Media

Social media isn't free. The platforms themselves may be, but it's incredibly difficult to break through the social media noise without putting dollars behind the effort. Businesses that are serious about social media allocate a budget for promoting their brands via posts and tweets. Facebook has admitted that only 16 percent of a page's followers will see a brand's unpaid post, but paying to promote scales this number significantly the more you spend and constantly target your posts.

Not every business needs to be on *every* social media platform. Don't dilute your efforts. Pick the ones that best serve your business's goals. What are the best channels to share the content you can create? Where are your audiences?

Even though social media feels like a place for the masses, ultimately your social media followers should feel like a close-knit community of "insiders"—people who are getting information tailored to them and they can't get it anywhere else.

Also, don't think of social media for "selling"—not directly. It's a place for content. Provide valuable content and you'll create fierce customer loyalty. Remember, we're humans and we can recognize selfish advertising, and so we'll be quick to un-follow, unlike, unpin, or run screaming into the hills.

Lastly, think of social media as essentially a 24/7 conversation, a conversation that will go on with or without you, one held among customers saying what they want about your brand, a conversation filled with potential customers who don't even know they want to hear about your brand. *Be a part of that conversation.* Hire someone to manage your social media, either an in-house person or an agency.

◀◀◀

Bottom Line

Knowing who you are and tailoring your image accordingly can be a springboard for personal and professional success, especially in the world of social media where in-person interaction is rare and where you could very well be interacting with thousands of people at once. It only takes one failed tweet to lose hundreds of followers.

7

Voice

Words mean more than what is set down on paper. It takes the human voice to infuse them with deeper meaning.
—Maya Angelou

It's a war zone in business nowadays. Terrified, territorial employees are all part of the fear-based workplace. When companies are announcing layoffs every week, it's no wonder that employees bury their collective heads in the sand. "If I can just disappear, I'll be safe," they've said to me. One day I got a call from a young executive saying, with relief, "Whew, I dodged the bullet again. My colleague just got zapped, but it was either him or me. I'm sorry for him, but at least I'm safe. For now...."

In this culture of fear, it's hard to have a voice. Everyone's so afraid of messing up and tripping on a landmine that no one wants to take a step. Everyone's so afraid to say the wrong thing, no one's speaking up, and no one's getting heard.

This is self-sabotage; all of it. It is powered by a real fear of an outside saboteur. But if you're not sharing your ideas, then you're not going to get anywhere.

Communication, or, more like it, miscommunication, is one of the main ways people sabotage themselves. Knowing how to effectively communicate your wants, knowing how to confront a person without offending that person, knowing how to compliment a person without sounding like you're pandering—these are essential for getting ahead.

I'm going to give you the basics of communication, but there's so much more that can be said on this topic that I can't include in this book—that would be a book unto itself! In fact, my last book, *Loud & Clear*, covers this topic completely. Here, I can only give you the basics of how to communicate when you're talking to anyone.

I'll help you find your voice and feel comfortable communicating in it, whether in speaking or in writing. When you have something behind what you're saying, when you have a foundation of confidence, built through preparation, education, and practice, you're going to feel much stronger speaking up. And when you can share your ideas with confidence, you will advance.

▶▶

Words From the Wise—Gee Rittenhouse, PhD
Vice President and General Manager,
Cloud and Virtualization for Cisco

Why Contact Matters

I form pretty tight bonds with the leadership team. It's not about just meeting monthly for business reviews or whatnot. We meet several times a day, at least once a week, to go through issues. I get a pretty good sense of things when I stay in contact with my team. I never see them go off the rail because the feedback group is way too tight for that. The interaction requires more work, but I get a better sense of what's going on with them and what outside their work may be affecting them. Perhaps it's something personal like looking for a house, or kids going to college in the fall. When I'm aware of these temporary things that may be affecting performance, I can understand why the person may be getting a bit overwhelmed. Then I can work to adjust things so we don't end up stretching the individual too fast, too hard.

◀◀

Word Out

Rick, a highly functional technology whiz kid, had whipped up a revolutionary invention and was ready to market the prototype. He was excited—overly excited about his technology, in fact—and that excitement manifested as arrogance. Also, he was scared because the success or failure of his company was riding on his ability to sell the product to potential investors.

In order to sell his invention to potential investors, Rick had to be able to explain the technology to people who weren't knowledgeable about technology and needed only to know how the product was going to make the consumer buy the product in order to make the investors rich.

Rick was so caught up in the pressure of selling and the uniqueness of the technology, he couldn't get out of his own head. He couldn't connect to his investors and make them feel connected to his product. His whole schtick was *Sell! Sell! Sell!* This served to extinguish any light bulbs that had gone off in his audience. Rick's supervisor had told him numerous times to stop yelling the sell and to listen to the investors who were interested, but had turned off because of Rick blistering them with his "sell."

I had videotaped Rick's presentation and showed it to him later. I pointed out how, because he was scared, he ended up badgering his audience. He was losing sales because he couldn't grasp the moment he had won his audience. He was in desperate need of analyzing his audience's needs and of creating a story that would bring the product to life.

Everyone's needs are unique. It's important for you to learn what works for you to get your word out and help you win the deal, whatever that deal is, whether you're wooing investors or giving a wedding toast.

It's on You

"I can't make a presentation unless I've had a few drinks," a young female executive confided to me one night at a networking event. Here was a bright, educated, attractive, well-put-together woman in her late 20s who was terrified of "being exposed" during a presentation without the shelter of alcohol. She, like so many people, felt like she was totally transparent when up in front of peers, or briefing customers on business solutions. She felt that somehow the audience will be able to literally see through her and detect her lack of confidence; that the audience would know immediately what her insecurities were and jump on them to humiliate her.

In doing so, she was giving her power over to the audience. Instead of commanding them, she was letting them intimidate her, for reasons her own insecurities made up for her in her head. Tip: Most people will give you the benefit of the doubt; they actually *want* to like you.

The primary reason we give up our power to the audience is that we have not spent the time trying to analyze the who, what, where, when, and why of the occasion. We feel we are suddenly transparent; the audience can literally see our flaws and absolutely knows our failings. We're exposed, vulnerable, and standing in front of the firing squad.

Speaking in public is a huge issue for people of all ages, no matter the amount of education or experience. It's such a huge issue that it is still considered the number one fear, ahead of fear of dying. But it doesn't have to be like that.

All Communication Is "Presentation"

I am constantly amazed every time I receive a panic call from a client asking for help at the last minute—and I do mean last minute, sometimes only hours before an event—because the presenters slated to speak at televised regulatory hearings or corporate board meetings were ill-prepared. We get lost in the tactics of preparing the presentation and forget what the audience needs. And the sad truth is that it takes but 30 minutes or less of preparation to get to know an audience in advance of the presentation.

If you're not convinced that strong communication skills are important, then let's take an extreme situation: you're about to have a surgical procedure where an anesthesiologist is going to inject you and put you to sleep for the duration. Talk about being out of control. If this chapter does nothing else to stir your desire to bulk up your communication skills, listen to this from a highly experienced anesthesiologist.

▶▶▶

Words From the Wise—Richard Armstrong, MD
Anesthesiologist, Horizon Family Medical

Lethal Lying
Information taken from the patient is very important to provide a safe anesthetic. The last intake of solid food and fluids, medications taken recently, smoking history, and drug and alcohol addiction history help us make the decisions regarding

treatment. The answers to these personal questions are the ones most uncomfortable for patients to share with us as caregivers, but if we get misinformation, the outcome can be lethal. For example, if a patient is dishonest about the last time they had a meal, he or she can aspirate. Separating natural nervousness from dishonesty is difficult, but if there is a question in my mind, I have to assume that his or her stomach is not empty or that more alcohol has been consumed than is being reported.

◄◄

Communication Pitfalls

Whether you're presenting to an audience of one or one thousand, the same guidelines apply, and many of the same obstacles will trip you up in getting your message across. Here are the four main communication potholes on the road to success:

1. You don't know where to begin when it's time to speak.
2. You don't paint a clear picture.
3. You let others interfere with or distort your message while you're delivering it; you're not prepared for the Q&A.
4. You don't let your personality come through—you don't SPARC-le.

Now let's look into how to fill them.

Know Your Audience

You don't know where to begin when it's time to speak.

If you don't know how you are going to end the journey for the audience, how can you possibly know where to begin? It's like taking your car out of the garage and aimlessly driving down the road in search of a destination.

I have developed this foolproof plan for communicating with an audience that can serve you effectively, whether you're speaking to one person or an audience of one thousand.

You know what you want from your audience. To get there, you need to find out what your audience needs/wants from *you*. How many times in my career have I heard employees, when asking for a raise, talk about why they need one? Business owners don't really care about why you feel you need a raise unless you can tell them how it is going to help their business.

You need to step back from what you want and take some time to analyze your audience. What are the benefits for your audience if he, she, or they accommodate your request?

You need to communicate in a way that is personalized, that's customized to that audience. There is no such thing as a one-size-fits-all approach to effective communication.

You need your audience to understand the information, especially if they are not from your team, your company or, for that matter, your industry. The person or persons receiving your message needs to know what you want them to do with the information. No one can read your mind about what you want, and that includes your spouse or partner.

Most importantly, you need to be able to motivate your audience to do what you want them to do with the information. In other words, how you present is as critical as what you present. You want your message to land on their shoulders, shake their shoulders, and get them out of their seats and doing what you wish them to do.

NAME	ATTITUDE	KNOWLEDGE	INTEREST	INFLUENCE
Ally	high	high	high	low
Adversary	low	low	low	medium
Neutral	low	low	high	high

Making a Power Map

This tool is most effective when you need to persuade a group about something, but it can also be used for a one-on-one discussion.

If you are presenting to 20 or fewer people, I suggest that you actually make a list using their names, and underneath their names, decide if that person is an ally, neutral, or adversary.

The next column is the level of interest. Here, write down to what degree the audience actually cares about your topic—low, medium, high—followed then by the level of knowledge of you, your company, your project, and, especially important, the level of influence that person has in his or her company/team/industry.

Next, write down the issues that you need to address in order to flip that person to your way of thinking or to motivate that person to act.

Finally, write down the key messages that develop from this map. What do all these people have in common? From that, you can begin to build your stories and examples, those elements that are going to help your audience really connect with your message.

Message Mapping

You don't paint a clear picture.

After you have analyzed what the audience needs from you, how you come across to people, now it's important to be sure that your audience will grab hold of your information, retain it, and act on it. To do this, I use a technique called Message Mapping.

A Message Map is a collection of bubbles consisting of random thoughts that you collect on a white board or sheet of paper. Once all these thoughts are out there, they can be collected and organized. The visual really helps.

In the center bubble, write down the bottom line for your audience; what your audience needs to hear to do what you want them to do. As indicated earlier, this should not really be more than 12 to 14 words. From there, create other bubbles that support that bottom line. These will become the elements of your message that help get your bottom line across. This needs to be a short sentence because you might not be presenting to the decision maker. Therefore, you want the person listening to you to remember the bottom line and be able to lift it wholesale and tell the decision maker. You never want your message to be corrupted by being too long or too obtuse.

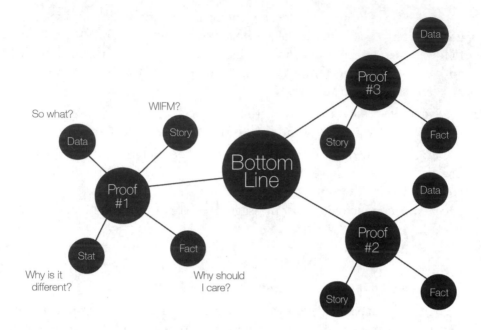

Anatomy of a Message

Before you craft any message to anyone, you have to ask yourself the three questions the audience is silently or directly asking you:

► So what?

► Who cares?

► What's in it for me? (WIIFM—my personal favorite.)

A message has three parts: A bottom line of no more than 12 to 14 words, proof, and "make me care." The bottom line is straightforward. It's the reason why you've called the meeting and what you hope to achieve from the meeting. The proof is the data—it's why this request you're making is essential, supported with facts. The "make me care" could be considered the warm, fuzzy part of a message. This element is critically important if your audience is not informed to the degree you might be in the technical aspects of the product or technology.

What you bring to the message is so important, whether you are giving a presentation to a group of people or one-on-one. This may come as a surprise to you, but the vast majority of what people remember a week after hearing a presentation is how that presenter looked and sounded, as well as his/her eye contact, gestures, and mood. In fact, a whopping 55 percent of what an audience remembers is the nonverbal.

Your voice and how you use it is 38 percent of what people remember: vocal projection, vocal quality, variations of volume, pitch of your voice, and pacing of your voice. Do you use signal phrases (for example, "This is important" or "If you remember nothing else, remember this") to pull in the attention of the audience? Do you pause to let the audience absorb the information and thereby bracketing off key messages?

Amazingly, only 7 percent of what your audience walks away with is the content of your message. That's why you have to work to focus your audience on the words you feel are important and not the other way around.

I've seen it happen so often: presenters leaving it up to the audience to decide what's important and what is not. That's the kiss of death. Pointing out what's important is the presenter's responsibility. You have to know that before going in.

▶▶▶

Words From the Wise—Grant Herman
Cloud Based Solutions Analyst at Booz Allen Hamilton

Working with Multiple Generations

Being a part of Generation Y is probably the most difficult position to be in. We live as schizophrenic human beings that must be humble and cocky at the same time. Older workers talk about or complain that junior staff is lazy and that we have no work ethic, which seems ridiculous considering that our generation has had to find a job in one of the toughest job markets since the Depression. Every day I feel resistance toward decisions that I make or ideas I have. I also feel like older generations had once been willing to mentor younger staff, but that way of engagement seems to be fading.

I have found that to diplomatically overcome these obstacles, you have to be polite but try to speak your ideas. You still need to remember that you are junior staff.

Here are three things I try to remember:

1. Younger employees, especially those who work in large, international companies, need to look at problems and try to solve them in the long term. I can't always do what is best for me right at that moment, but I need to have foresight.

2. If you don't like a staff member, junior or senior, you need to remain respectful, even if someone tries to provoke you. I always allow my work to speak for me.

3. Check your ego at the door. While I'm at work, my main objective needs to be doing what's best for my team/company.

There is a Taoist philosophy and martial arts style in which you are supposed to be like a cork in a bucket of water. No matter how many times you hit the cork, the cork will always bounce back. The harder you hit the cork, the faster it will bounce back. The youth at work must be like the cork in the bucket: buoyant.

◀◀

The Four Cornerstones of Communication

In my work in communications, I've discovered four elements that are essential in presenting a message:

1. Chemistry.
2. Credibility.
3. Clarity.
4. Consistency.

Chemistry

What makes a person persuasive? Remember in Chapter 3, in which we talked about charisma? It comes down to chemistry:

▶ Does that person like you?

▶ Do you like that person?

▶ What do you have in common?

▶ How can you bond with that person?

It's a well-known fact that people are attracted to those most like themselves. Therefore, if there is anything that is obvious about a person that you can tap into and use as a connector, you should use it. You don't know the person yet? Not a problem. You can find a considerable amount of information about people on the Internet these days.

Recently, I worked with someone who was about to fly off to the Middle East to present in front of a key government official. I asked my client, "How much do you know about him?"

"Not much."

"Well," I said, "let's see what we can find out about him on YouTube." With a click of a mouse, we found a video of the official, and watched it several times to study his body language and listen to how he spoke. It was golden. And now my globetrotting client uses social media as normal preparation for new deals and has tripled his revenue.

Credibility

Do you back up everything you say with proof? If you are saying that your company is a leader in a specific sector, you must give examples of how. An interesting fact about oral communication is that we tend to remember specifics in threes, the rhythm of threes. Therefore, if you could give three short examples—how your technology or equipment, for instance, will make that person's life easier, happier, and richer—they will remember you longer.

Clarity

Do you speak the same language as your audience, literally, in the global workplace? How can you communicate well in a language that isn't your native tongue? For the first 30 seconds, speak slowly. Then, when the audience tunes into the rhythm of your accent—and we all have an accent—they will continue to listen. Because if we are playing catch up with a speaker and can't understand some of the words, we typically tune out.

This cornerstone of clarity also refers to techno speak or alphabet soup, the use of acronyms. If your tendency is to use techno speak, I suggest that the first time you use a term, say the complete word and then say, "From this point on, I'll refer to it as..." and use the acronym.

When people can't understand you, it isn't just about the words you're using. Vocal tics will bring you down. Using too many "ums," "ers," and "you knows" will distract your audience. Upspeak, meaning when you express a statement, it comes out sounding like a question, will make people believe you're not confident about what you're saying; they'll tune you out thinking, "Why should I believe what this person is telling me if this person doesn't even believe it?" Maybe we shouldn't judge people by their idiosyncrasies, but the reality is that we do.

So many people mess up perfectly manageable situations with their poor choice of words. Earlier this year, Tim Armstrong of AOL was planning on making changes to the 401(k) contributions, which he justified by giving bad examples and using the term "distressed babies." That day, the price of AOL shares was $49.49. A couple of days later, it fell to $47.28. Armstrong e-mailed his employees the following day, apologizing and stating he would not make changes to the 401(k) contributions. By Monday, the story had made its way to the media and the stock price dropped to $45.76 and has been slowly declining since then. At the time of this writing (June 2014), it had tumbled to $36.36. Perhaps had Armstrong used a less insensitive term, the stock would not have been affected.

The other way people mismanage their words is that they do not speak or write correctly. Do you know when to use "fewer" and when to use "less?" What's the difference between "farther" and "further?" Do you think using the term "irregardless" is correct? How about using the phrase "these ones" to point out a group or collection? (Hint: "Less" is unquantifiable. There is less sand on the beach. "Fewer" is within scope. There are fewer pebbles there. "Further" is abstract. You're going to further your education. And "farther" implies a measurable distance. You have to go farther than the next town to get to the school.)

There's also a tendency for people to be too casual with their language. Instead of saying an elegant "you're welcome," when someone pays a compliment or a favor, people tend to slide into a lazy "no worries" or "no problem." Speak correctly and people will take you more seriously. Trust me!

Finally, the golden rule of speaking: the drama happens during the silence. Build it in strategically. This isn't meant for when you've lost your way, though you might have but for different reasons. Make the silence, the pause, count. There is nothing quite so powerful and riveting for an audience.

Warming Up

I don't care if you're auditioning for a Broadway show or needing to call the dean at your school. You need to sound good when you speak! Whether you're a performer or briefcase-toting business person, you need to gently warm up your voice every day before conducting meetings whether by phone or in person. Here are some tips performers rely on to release their star-power mojo:

- ▶ *Humming up and down the musical scale.* Not loud, but gently, quietly warming up the muscles of the larynx (voice box).

- ▶ *Making the BRRRRR sound*—if you can't do it, there's tension. This loosens up your mouth for easy articulation. The same goes for making a motorboat sound or trilling like a cat—just with the tongue. You want to loosen your mouth to communicate well.

- ▶ *Say "Tip of the tongue the teeth the lips"* three times quickly and really accentuate the words. This helps your facial muscles. If you find you're being sloppy articulating the words, start over.

- ▶ *Yawn.* This relaxes the throat and the face. Drop your jaw and let your tongue hang out and soon you will begin to yawn. (Just don't do this during the meeting or audition. Please.)

- ▶ *Here's a great tip for speaking in a noisy venue,* like a crowded restaurant. Speak through your nose. Your voice will carry, it will not hurt your vocal cords, and no one will detect that you are speaking with a nasal tone. This is a lifesaver for singers and public speakers.

Also, you want to keep your body relaxed physically. Before you have your meeting, do jumping jacks, run in place, anything to get the blood flowing—even doing pushups against the wall in the lavatory!

▶▶

Words From the Wise—Samantha Stroh Bailey
Professional Writer and Editor

Grammar Matters

After almost 20 years of teaching grammar and writing and editing countless manuscripts, I come across very similar errors that often stump the most talented of writers. Here are the top errors I find.

Past vs. passed: Once you know the rules for these, you'll have an easier time deciding which is correct.

Past

"Past" can be used as an adjective, noun, preposition, or adverb.

Adjective: "All of her past boyfriends were criminals." Here, "past" is used to modify the noun "boyfriends."

Noun: "It is often better not to dwell on the past."

Preposition: "It is 20 past five." "Past" is used to indicate time. "The place where he was murdered is one block past the park." Here, "past" indicates location.

Adverb: "She ran past his house every day to get a glimpse of him." Here, "past" is used to modify the verb "ran."

Passed

"Passed" is the past tense form of the verb "to pass." For example: "He passed by her just as she bent over and her pants ripped." And: "They slowed down as they passed the accident."

Lie vs. Lay: This has got to be one of the most asked questions I get as an editor. It all has to do with the direct object, which is the thing or person in a sentence which receives the action of the verb.

"I write a book."

"I kiss his face."

"I eat pizza."

"I walk to work."

Book, face, pizza, and work are all direct objects.

Present Tense:

"I lie down, exhausted from the previous night." Lie does not need a direct object.

"I lay the documents on the table and stare at him."

"She lay her daughter down in the crib, filled with a joy she could not contain." Lay requires a direct object because you need to lay something or someone down. (Hint: Think of the prayer, "Now I lay me down to sleep.")

Past Tense:

This is not an easy one. There are three forms for every verb—present, past, past participle, shown as follows:

Present: Lie.

Past: Lay.

Past Participle: Lain.

"I lay down, exhausted from the previous night, and curled up in a ball."

"She had lain down five hours earlier, and when she woke up, she was startled to realize that so much time had gone by."

"I laid the documents on the table and stared at him."

"Before he stormed off, I had laid the documents on the table and stared at him."

"She laid her daughter in the crib, filled with a joy she could not contain."

"Once she had laid her daughter in the crib, filled with a joy she could not contain, she cried for the mother she never had."

◀◀

Consistency

The fourth cornerstone is consistency. Do you know people who promise a lot and don't deliver? We all know people who say they will complete a task and somehow don't. Consistency is a very key trait in a persuasive person. We have to trust that a person is going to come through before we decide to help a person. Your boss has to trust that you can handle the added responsibility if she or he is going to promote you. Or if you're trying to convince someone to support a cause, he or she has to believe that you too have reliably and consistently helped that cause.

▶▶▶

Words From the Wise—Andre Mechaly
Marketing and Strategy Director,
Network and Infrastructure Systems at Thales

It's How You Say It

Technical experts sometimes have some difficulty explaining things to non-experts. Most people can't leave home without their smart phones but they don't care about a smart phone's quad-processor at 1.5 GHz. How do we explain these technical things so that users understand what the challenge is and why our solution is better than the competition? One of the best compliments I have ever gotten after a speech was from a non-technical expert who thanked me for my speech, telling me he really felt he understood everything I was explaining.

I remember having to speak at a sales conference about mobile data traffic explosion to show sales people that all the usage people were having with video on their smart phone would lead to terrific amounts of data that would need enhanced networks offering opportunities for business for the company. While preparing the presentation, I wanted to tell my audience that mobile data traffic would reach 50 exabytes by 2015. Few of us know what an exabyte is and probably even fewer can explain what it represents. To explain that, I computed how many smart phones we need to stack given their memory capacity to reach that amount of data. It appears that when you stack smart phones of 32 gigabytes (GB) of data, once the stack's height reach 1.25 the diameter of earth, you reach 50 exabytes. When making my presentation and explaining about that amount of data, I invited my audience to play together and stack their smart phones which they started to do. I then told them that I'd leave them, and that they should ring me once the height is over earth's diameter. Everybody laughed; each of them today knows what an exabyte is!

◀◀◀

Storytelling

Human beings are storytellers, way back to the days of cavemen writing with pictures on walls of caves. We relate to that which we can see in our mind's eye. Have you ever read a book you loved and then went to see the film made from the book? Did you leave the theater feeling disappointed? Why is that? The picture you created in your mind based on the actions in the book are perfect; you created them. Then at the movies, someone else represented that story; therefore, very often your perception of the story gets sabotaged.

Having spent decades preparing executives for presentations, I always marvel at why presentations become so sterile. I remember sitting through a medical conference of 3,000 distracted physicians all there to learn the latest in medical treatment for serious diseases. I watched the doctors during some of the dry, tedious, PowerPoint lectures. They were either texting each other or their families, doing the daily crossword puzzle in the local newspaper (I'm not kidding), yawning, or plain out sleeping.

Then, as soon as the speaker said, "Let me tell you about a patient I treated who..." 3,000 pairs of eyeballs suddenly fixed on the speaker. The audience was about to hear a story, and that's what got their attention.

A story told in 100 words or less can drive home the message far better than 3,000 words explaining the treatment. Do we need both? Yes, but pepper your presentations with examples, anecdotes, and personal experiences. People want to know *you*. You are the delivery system of your message. Otherwise, what initially happened to the speaker at the medical conference will also happen to you.

Develop what you want to say as a story using the five W's: who, what, where, when, and why. If you can answer these questions, you'll be able to create examples, stories that will inspire your audience and sell your product, idea, or service.

People you're presenting to may say "I hear you," but as soon as you bring your presentation to life, they'll say, "Oh, I see." They are now viewing the story in their mind's eye, which then locks in your message and your success.

Controlling Interests

You let others interfere with or distort your message while you're delivering it; you're not prepared for the Q&A.

Anyone you're delivering a message to can hijack it at any point in your delivery. This is not an ideal situation for you, especially because it means that, once control of the message is lost, you're not going to get what you want—you're going to have to acquiesce to what someone else wants.

Not everyone wants you to succeed. You may have a boss that wants to hold you back because he or she likes you in the position you're in. You're handling things for that person. You're doing such a great job that he or she couldn't possibly promote you or even manage if you went off to run another department! So, yes, sometimes you are held back because you are too good. And the person holding you back will distort what you're trying to express by blowing sunshine and praise at you and letting you know just how valuable you are! You cannot let that happen.

Another reason why someone will try and derail you is that what you want is in direct opposition to what they want. How do you disagree without sniping or pandering? Use "bridge" terms that can guide the conversation back to your agenda, like, "Let me build on that" or "Maybe I can add...." And here is a bridging term no one can argue with: "In my experience...." This phrase should work when you're defending your point of view, your research, or your decisions.

Remember, another person's agenda is only your concern in the way that it can throw you off of yours. You have to keep control of the conversation if you want to succeed.

Here are a few more bridging terms:

- ► That's an important point because what I am discovering is...
- ► I'm not familiar with that, but what I can tell you is...
- ► Actually...

▶▶

Words From the Wise—Art Stevens
Cofounder, StevensGouldPincus

Listen!

The primary way people sabotage themselves in negotiations and new business pitches is by not listening. Dialog should never be about "me, me, me." That approach will turn off a new business prospect faster than you can talk. It should be about "you, you, you," and you can only invite the person across the table to share his needs and issues with you if you truly listen.

There is a huge difference between being articulate and being talky. The articulate professional can convey much meaning in a few words. Less is more.

The best way to have a successful, sabotage-free negotiation is to not draw lines in the sand. Everything should be on the table and should remain there. Both parties should remain transparent, calm, civil, and amenable. Inflexibility is the surest way to send all parties packing and ensure your own defeat. As a professional "matchmaker," it's my job to keep both sides interested, excited, positive, and focused. If both parties can be persuaded that by working together they can create something wonderful, there will be more willingness to give in on small things.

◀◀◀

"Half-Life" Exercise

As Art says, there is a difference between being articulate and talky. This is especially important when you develop your "elevator pitch," that quick assessment of who you are and what you do which you need to deliver in the amount of time it takes to travel in an elevator with someone you've never met before, someone who wants to know something about you.

When the time you have to capture someone's interest is limited, you have to make every word count. Try this exercise to help you eliminate unnecessary words that can distract your audience from listening to you.

First:

1. Have a stopwatch, timer, or smartphone with stopwatch or timer option ready.
2. Have a recording device ready.
3. Have your pitch ready.

Now, set your device for 60 seconds and record your pitch. Play it back. Where are the unnecessary words? Cut them out.

Next, set your device for 30 seconds and record your pitch. Again, target any words that are unnecessary and slowing you down and cut them from your pitch.

Finally, set your device for 30 seconds and record your pitch one last time. Listen. This should be the one.

I guarantee that you will find the nucleus of your message through this exercise.

Half-Life Exercise

Try delivering your message in:

o 60-seconds

o 30-seconds

o 15-seconds

Shining Through

You don't let your personality come through—you don't SPARC-le.

So many people get so stressed out about presenting a message, they become wooden and stilted. This is not a great way to bring people over to your side. No one wants to engage with a marionette except a puppeteer; and you don't want to be controlled by a puppeteer!

It's okay to let your personality shine through, especially when it comes to an interview, audition, or any situation in which you're selling yourself. The person doing the hiring wants to know you have the right credentials to perform the task correctly, but a person also wants to know that they can work with someone, daily, under pressure, under deadlines. People bring you aboard because they like you. Without knowing how you really are, how can they know if they like you or not?

There are ways to give your point of view and still keep your job. I have a friend who is brilliant, outspoken, and unemployed. I believe the sole reason for this is his way of phrasing his comments. He insults rather than inspires. If this sounds familiar to you, try recording your comments when chatting with someone on the phone. There's no law that I know of against your recording your own voice, just don't record your colleague's voice without getting permission. Play back the recording. If *you* are insulted by your word choices and tone of voice, you can bet your audience will be as well. You should be able to offer your point of view phrased in a way that is inclusive rather than divisive.

How to Handle an Interview

At the time this book is being written, the global job market is on the uptick. The bad news is those who have been underemployed or unemployed are so desperate that they might sabotage themselves in the interview. You don't want to sabotage yourself before you've even made it through the front door!

There are laws in certain countries about the types of questions that are off limits, such as your age, your religion, and your lifestyle. However, I have reports and personal experience of even U.S. companies asking those off limits questions. And, if you are interviewing for companies based outside of the U.S., many of those countries do not have such laws. Therefore, you must be prepared and decide whether or not to answer the questions.

From my survey of people seeking new opportunities, many of them are choosing to answer the questions. And here's why. Employers know they are in the power seat and have hundreds of candidates lining up outside their doors. They, unfortunately, may decide to ask what they want. You need to be prepared if this happens with answers you can comfortably express so that you do not feel sucker-punched.

In the employer's defense, what they see on your resume does not reflect who you are. Who are you really? Are you honest and ethical? Are you someone the employer and your direct manager want to be around? Do you have anything in common?

You can decide not to answer the question, but at the very least you must have something in your arsenal to bridge your way out of a sticky situation. For example:

Question: What is your religion?

Bridge: I'd rather not say, however...

Answer: I have a strong moral compass. I am highly ethical, believe in your company's values, and am dedicated to protecting them.

Whether for a media interview, job interview, or audition for a show, you have to at least acknowledge the question even if you can't or won't directly answer it, otherwise your credibility will be compromised.

Bridging

- ► Answer the question.
- ► Then, bridge to what you want to talk about.
- ► Use "for example," "and," "however."

Handling a Tricky Interviewer

Interviews and auditions are conducted by human beings, not robots, so you can't count on the person interviewing you being even and robotic. Here are some tricky types of interviewers and some tips for handling them:

Rapid fire: You have to break the rhythm of the speaking pattern. Breathe; speak slowly and methodically to break the tempo.

Caustic: Use the bridging word "actually." It diffuses emotion. For instance:

Question: Why haven't you had a job for the last three years?

Answer: Actually, I have spent that time volunteering for the local hospital, taking continuing education courses at my local college, and tutoring needy children.

You can deflect the accusation with something, anything, other than "I've been looking for a job."

Sarcastic: This is the interviewer who wants to make you feel bad about yourself. For example:

Question: I'm surprised you aren't more up to date with your tech skills. Why aren't you?

Answer: I am willing to learn anything you feel is important on my own time. The skills I have listed are what my previous employer designated as important.

Trying to Trip You Up: Yes, sometimes the interviewer only wants you to fail. This person may be bored with their job or may be feeling bullied by their situation. They need a place to exert their power and, lucky you, you are going to be the target of all their dashed dreams and career frustrations!

The idea is that you answer the person's question or acknowledge the person's complaint but, then, with one of the bridging phrases, move to *your* message and then *stop talking*. In other words, once you cross the bridge, *blow it up*, meaning do not circle back to the questioner's point of view. If you do, it is likely your adversary will continue badgering you and you'll end up feeling defensive and defeated. The key is that you must at least acknowledge the questioner's concern before you bridge to your side of the argument.

When someone tries to bully you into giving an answer or agreeing to something you don't want to agree to, there are ways to answer and remain neutral.

First, it's better to have both people sit down rather than the bully standing over you. Next, let the person vent without saying anything. After about 15 minutes, the person will run out of steam, and then you begin slowly and quietly speaking. While that person is venting, you sit calmly and slowly breathe in and out. Focus on your breathing.

Now, here are some phrases you can use to bridge the conversation back on track:

- ▶ We've talked about this before...
- ▶ Let's clarify...
- ▶ Help me understand where you're going with this...

▶ I don't remember asking for your opinion on this... (Note: This is important to say in a friendly, not caustic, way.)

▶ I wonder what motivates you to talk this way to me...

How to Ruin an Interview

Here are a few ways you can often sabotage yourself during an interview or audition:

▶ Call attention to your insecurity with ungainly body language or facial tics or both.

▶ Don't look anyone in the eye.

▶ Greet your interviewer with a limp handshake.

▶ Be sure to point out that you're tired, have a sore throat, you don't interview well, etc.

▶ Be unprepared—just wing it!

▶ Continue to apologize throughout the interview about all of the previous points.

The Bottom Line

Actually, being prepared takes less effort than making excuses. You want to plan what you want to say, and you want to rehearse what you're going to say before you deliver your message. Though I have seen in my experience that over-rehearsing can be disastrous, you want to know what those words sound like before they fall out of your mouth. Videotape yourself (see Chapter 6). Be confident that you know your stuff and you're saying it well before you open your mouth to speak.

8

Aptitude

Think before you speak. Read before you think.
—Fran Lebowitz

Are you curious? Answer the following questions "true" or "false":

1. Every day I wake up and wonder what new adventure might await.
2. I marvel at the vast differences in people and want to learn what makes them tick.
3. I try to learn one new word each day just because it's fun.
4. When I take in the news of the day, I move beyond my TV or newspaper and do more background reading on something I read or hear that intrigues me.
5. I engage at least one person a day in conversation that isn't centered on my needs.

If you answered any of the above questions "false," it's time to get your curiosity back in check! Welcome to Aptitude.

My mother grew up being called "nebby," which is Scotch-Irish for "nosey." She had an intense curiosity about everything. Well into her late 70s, she decided to learn everything there was to know about football because she was getting tired of not understanding what all the Denver Bronco fans around her were always talking about. "If you can't lick 'em, join 'em," was her mantra. There was no Internet at the time; she had to go to the library to read everything she could. Oh, and she had macular degeneration and could only see with her peripheral vision. But that didn't stop her. Her curiosity, her desire to learn, was insatiable. Ultimately, she became a huge Broncos fan and remained one until the day she died in her late 80s.

I inherited that sense of curiosity from her. I can't imagine traveling through life without looking around and wondering about things. It could be something so seemingly ordinary, like the pattern of bark on a Norwegian Elm, or the cloud formations in the summer sky. Even cracks in the sidewalk intrigue me and make me want to learn more about the world and all the little details that make it work. Not everyone is like this, though my worry is about people who have no curiosity at all.

Curiosity and a desire to learn are essential to your success. People who go through life with their nose pressed to the grindstone don't get anything out of life. They live like machines that perform their function, burn out, and then get replaced by new machines.

I want more than that for you!

In this chapter, I will show you how to embrace your sense of curiosity and nurture it. I'm going to coach you to use that sense of curiosity we're all born with to go after the knowledge you need to get ahead.

I'm not saying it's time to leave your job and go back to school. There are so many ways you can expand your mind (and your horizons) and in just minutes a day. It all starts with training yourself to become curious again.

▶▶

Words From the Wise—Michael Mastro
Broadway Actor/Director/Career Coach

Building Your Brain

I've become increasingly interested in the creative power of the human mind. Over the last century, numerous philosophies, teachings, books—whole movements—have appeared with the purpose of awakening people to the remarkable power of thought and intention. Some are more rational in tone, and some are more mystical/miracle-minded in their thinking. Either way, science has proven that a person's mental focus and patterns of thought absolutely affect his or her autonomic nervous system. This, in turn, affects the way we feel and experience life during the course of our days, and that monumentally affects our energy levels, our sense of well-being, and ultimately, the way we interact with the world. Our successes in that world are deeply dependent upon the quality of our interaction with it. Research some of these practices and see what works for you.

I encourage any personal work that helps us to take full responsibility for our minds and the way we use them. Prayer and meditation are age-old practices, but exploring the use of other more recently developed practices, like affirmative thought, hypnosis, visualization, Emotional Freedom Techniques (tapping), and so forth, can lead to a more conscious ownership of one's mind, and to the responsible and creative use of it.

◄◄◄

Curiosity Killed the...Self-Sabotage

Yes, it's true. Curious people do not self-sabotage themselves. Curious people grow in knowledge and experience, and as a result, in success.

Years ago, I had some friends, the Dibbles, whose curiosity of all places known was so great that they devoted all their free time to travel. In their home, a 10-foot-by-12-foot map of the world hung on the wall, and every few months one of them would close their eyes and stick a pin into the map to decide their next trip. By the time they hit their 70s, they had traveled most everywhere.

They'd come back from these long trips, sometimes three months long, and put together a slide show, which they called "Dibble Logs," that they shared with the community.

I always found the Dibbles' curiosity about the world so remarkable. They started the process by sticking a pin in a map, but once they knew where they were headed, they took great pride in learning everything they could about the culture, the country, and the customs—and this was way before the Internet. That means they had to research the old-fashioned way, with hours spent in libraries and bookstores, as well as taking classes. Well into their later years, they had the spirit of two five-year-olds, eager to learn and discover.

There have been many studies done about this phenomenon, and there are many places to point the finger of blame as to where our curiosity gets killed. Maybe it's parents not wanting to answer so many questions. Maybe it's schools "force-feeding" one-size-fits-all curricula. Whatever kills curiosity, the good news is that you can get it back!

SPARC Words

The following words are designed to help "SPARC" curiosity in you. Notice how different these words are from the self-sabotage words of Chapter 1. Each day, choose a new SPARC word to give that curiosity of yours a jump start! We'll be using these in the Curiosity Challenge (next).

- ► Exercise.
- ► Practice.
- ► Dream.
- ► Connect.
- ► Believe.
- ► Listen.
- ► Hug.
- ► Celebrate.
- ► Communicate.
- ► Adjust.
- ► Uncover.
- ► Laugh.
- ► Review.
- ► Vocalize.
- ► Reflect.
- ► Dare.
- ► Envision.
- ► Imagine.
- ► Gratitude.
- ► Ponder.
- ► Strategize.
- ► Discover.
- ► Grin.

The Curiosity Challenge

Ask "why." "Why" is a much better question than "What?" "What" delineates the non-curious. Most of what passes for learning in our school systems essentially kills off kids' curiosity by only asking them to memorize the "What." I remember in school having to memorize dates of world events, not what sparked them; the "What" as opposed to the "Why." The road to reinvention starts with "Why."

Start curious. Write down the first thought that pops into your head in the morning. Whatever it is, however banal it seems, spend 10 minutes researching that thought online. For example, maybe you think it's time to throw back the bed sheets. Great! So go find out: Where did bed sheets originate? Which country, which century? Small, everyday, seemingly unimportant things can ignite our inherent curiosity and start re-training us to think rather than just act.

Find a SPARC word and stick with it. Each day, choose one word from the previous list. Take five minutes to do some research on it and then make it your focus for the day.

Don't be a "surface shopper." Always try to dig for the hidden meaning—nothing ever happens just on the surface. Do you remember the magazine *Highlights for Children*? I used to love to read that with my son when he was young. We especially enjoyed the sections on finding hidden pictures. That's what you should be looking for in every aspect of your life—all the "hidden pictures." The more you seek them out, the more they will reveal themselves to you.

If it ain't broke.... Well, even if it is, don't throw it out right away. Maybe you have an appliance that's broken beyond repair. Before you toss it, learn from it. Consider taking it apart and seeing what's inside. Pick one part and research its function, then move on to the next part. Who knows? What you learn might actually lead to you fixing it or fixing another thing that breaks down the line.

Do the "leg work." If you have a habit of asking the neighborhood trivia expert every time you need an answer to a question, try instead to figure it out on your own. What you learn will stick in your memory much better than grabbing the first answer you hear. For example, if you take a trip and have someone else make all the arrangements for you, you just go along for the ride. However, if you take a trip that you planned, adding to the itinerary your choice of hotel and restaurants, what a richer experience that trip will be for you!

Independence is a great asset to acquire, and one that having curiosity can gift to you. Start small. Go to a movie and when you come home, look up information about the location where the movie was shot, or see if you can find information about how the movie was made. When you go to a restaurant, ask questions about what's being offered on the menu.

Always force yourself to seek out more about any given thing, even if you already feel satisfied that you have enough information. Push past "satisfied" and stuff yourself with knowledge. Every day, you should be able to turn at least one "huh?" into a "huzzah!"

Let your curiosity wander, explore your universe, and you'll become more empowered and assured—both strong antidotes for self-sabotage.

The Meek Inherit Nothing

I've seen many people give over their power to someone in charge, in many different ways. When it comes to aptitude, we sometimes become complacent in our life; we get tired of growing and expanding our experiences, of enhancing our creativity, and instead we hand it over to a mentor, teacher, coach, boss, or partner. We give up; we lose our way. And we rely on someone else to fill in the blanks.

Sometimes the situation is more insidious; sometimes these people, who we trust to look after us, sort of come in and take over for us. It's happened to me all through my life and to many of my colleagues, clients, and friends.

Sometimes we only need mentors for a certain time and need to move on before this happens. Those heroes whom we've placed on pedestals are ordinary human beings, fallible and imperfect. They may be talented in a specific skill and possess knowledge we feel we deeply need, but once we learn that skill, we need to cut the cord—not toss them out of our life, but move on.

A good mentor knows that, too. A good leader doesn't knock your legs out from under you so you need to lean on that person to walk; he or she shows you how to make your legs stronger, how to use them in ways you never imagined possible, and sends you on your way.

When you don't move on, when you don't continue your quest to learn new things and grow, you burn out, become complacent, or stall in a job, industry, or skill that you have long since outgrown. The worst case scenario is that you begin to bend or curtail your ability in order to contort yourself into the job. I have witnessed hundreds of such victims of this kind of self-sabotage, riddled with fear to jump industries, but burnt out and ineffective in their current profession.

At some point we all need a reality check. Do you now know as much as your teacher knows? Is it time to move on?

▶▶▶

"Why Not?"—Phong Vu
Partner, Consumer-Driven 6-Sigma Management Institute

I was born in 1951, in North Vietnam. My mom, a school teacher, brought my sister and me up by herself until 1955, when the winds of war brought us to South Vietnam. We were re-united with my dad there. As the war intensified in 1968, my parents gave me a one-way ticket out of the country to Europe. A year later, I ended up in the U.S., where I (and most people in the world) thought would be a land of opportunities.

My life in America started in California. I worked as a busboy while attending college. Life was way better than back in Vietnam (you could get killed there). The tough part was learning to master the English language. I realized that until I could master the language, I would not succeed. I graduated in 1974 as an electrical engineer. My last year in college, I was a student Senator (my English got better).

I got married to my college girlfriend (I'm still with her now) and worked in San Francisco. In April of 1975, South Vietnam fell to the communist North. I went back to Saigon (now Ho Chi Minh City) to bring my family out of the battle-ravaged city. We escaped on one of the last helicopters lifting off from the U.S. Embassy in Saigon. I was moved by the bravery and unselfishness of the U.S. service men and women who saved and served the refugees and decided to join the U.S. Marines Reserve upon my return from Saigon. I subsequently served 12 years and was discharged as a Major.

After my officer training in the Marines, I worked at Ford Motor Company in Dearborn, Michigan, and worked my way to be leader of several major car and truck programs and became the Quality Director for Ford Global Truck Operations and then Six Sigma Global Deployment Director for Ford. I retired from Ford in 2003 and opened my own consultant business serving large corporations.

After all these years, I am grateful I came to America where I believe that one can still achieve one's goal if one is willing to plan and prepare for it. My life has been guided by some sage advice given to me by some very kind people. I still follow it.

My advice is to set a goal and stay with it. Look forward, learn from mistakes, and then move on. No deposit, no return. Always look at the glass half full ,so you have the energy to press on regardless of how tough things may be. Share and celebrate every small victory.

◄◄

"On the Job" Learning

I remember one of my managers early on in my career being "hands-off" in the extreme, but at the same time demanding excellence. For a new hire, that's sabotage waiting to happen. What I did was seek out people in the organization who seemed to know a particular skill and asked them. You'd be surprised how willing people are to share information, especially when they don't feel threatened (for example, competing with you for promotion or wage increase).

One of my most successful clients has long nurtured a network of people that she trusts to fill in the knowledge gaps that she personally doesn't have. She isn't afraid to hang out with other strong individuals because she well knows that doing so helps you address your weak side.

We tend to associate with people like ourselves, but that's not always in our best interest. I'm not saying don't associate with people who are like you; just don't be afraid to associate yourself with people who aren't. Those are the people who are going to fill in those gaps for you, not just tell you what you want to hear.

Work It Out

When it comes down to it, managers are human beings too. Some might be better at their roles of training and fostering talent and helping it to grow. Others may be less secure about their staff members becoming too strong, too smart. You can think that's not your issue, it's theirs, but in reality, it is your issue. If a manager doesn't realize that helping you develop is part of their role, or, worse, they are intentionally and willfully doing all they can to hold you back so they can keep you under their control, you have to do something about it.

I would definitely suggest that it needs to start with a conversation, and you're the one who needs to initiate that conversation. (See Chapter 7 for more information.)

Are you the "critical talent" in your organization? Should you be?

▶▶

Words From the Wise—Parinaz Sekechi
Learning Consultant, Alcatel-Lucent University

Understanding Critical Talent

I interact with business and HR leaders who identify critical talent. Critical talents are those people who have a unique set of skills that not everybody else has and are vital to the company. They have unique skills or knowledge critical to the success of business and difficult to replace from any employee population or function. But they are not necessarily part of the leadership pipeline and need specific nurturing to help them stay engaged. People who consistently exceed expectations are the people that will most likely get engaged, because they have such a wonderful success record of paying attention to their own development.

There is a growing trend toward learner-centric learning, where technology is used to deliver education on the learner's terms, enabling learners to access learning when it's needed. This is an approach near and dear to me. In the Alcatel-Lucent University, we have My Personal Learning Environment (My PLE) platform set up in such a way that you don't have to actually sit through each and every module. You can go straight to what we call "proof of competency," which is a quiz associated with the learning modules. If you pass the proof of competence, you go to the next proficiency level. We have found that this helps productivity because people aren't wasting time going through modules when they have the knowledge already. They can take a proof of competency and move on.

Another aspect to this platform is the social learning, the online community of learning which we map to competency areas, so there's a lot of engagement, information exchange, and learning from each other. This peer learning is one of the most exciting elements of My PLE platform. Based on my observation and experience, I truly believe peer learning reinforces knowledge transfer, helps form bonds within our global employee population, and can lead to increased morale and productivity. As part of this approach, I facilitate sessions with leaders who are role models and invite our critical talents to come and hear what it is that makes this particular leader successful, so well respected, and highly regarded.

For me, personally, having a diverse background and experience in understanding the value of relationships gives me the flexibility to help our leaders to see the difference between what they think they need and what is actually needed—which at the end of the day is how we can best support our employees to have a positive impact on the organization and achieve business success. Employees are the foundation for creating value in a company. Therefore, managers and leaders play an important role in inspiring, engaging, retaining, and attracting talent.

◀◀◀

Planning Your Re-Education

You don't have to wait for someone to tell you what you need to do. You don't need your manager to plot your course when it comes to learning. In fact, at a company that is hierarchical, controlling, demanding, or all three, where you need approval to take courses, I'd say go forward on your time, not the company's. Never risk sabotaging yourself because you're stumped at how to better yourself.

We can all continue learning. There is so much to learn out there and there isn't always a hefty tuition involved. If we are stalled at our job, housebound caring for ailing parents or young children or both, there is a wealth of free—*free!*—online courses from reputable universities called Massive Open Online Courses or MOOC. (MIT and Stanford offer them. Check the Internet for others.)

Or you can steal an hour away from daily burdens and go to your public library. Most offer free or inexpensive classes in everything from business writing to computer technology, so there is really no excuse for any one of us nowadays to go wanting in updating our technical skills and stimulating our curiosity.

The older you get, the more life experience you have. Whatever grit you have doesn't have to end once you retire. Today, even when you retire—especially when you retire—your life experience is of great value to universities. A whole new life could open for you. For example, a client of mine, upon retiring from his advertising job, began teaching at the continuing education school of his local university. He received a stipend for his work, but the main benefit to him was the free access to any of their classes. Through that, he developed his love of photography and a few years later opened an art gallery.

▶▶▶

Words From the Wise—Byron Gilliam
Head of U.S. trading for Olivetree Securities

Take Risks but Know Who You're Dealing With

If you're deciding between career options when you get out of school, take the one that is the biggest stretch. Do something crazy if you can.

My first job out of college was with a floor broker on the German exchange, conducted mostly in German. I had taken two years of German in college, but was barely conversational when I started. The job was rapid-fire stock trading in the pre-Internet era: a telephone on each ear and shouting at colleagues. Looking back, I wonder how I did it. Later on in life, I spent a year at a French stock broker in France. I thought I'd pick up French like I did German, but it never happened.

I've had jobs in four different countries (so far) and communication has been distinctly different in each. The Germans are no-nonsense, as you'd imagine them to be. You're expected to say what you think, with no penalties for disagreements. This suited me fine and I did well in that environment. When I moved to England, I continued to speak my mind openly and everyone would agree with me all the time. Then I found out that they were just agreeing to my face and keeping their real opinion to themselves. But it worked for me; people liked my candor and I stood out from others. When I got back to the United States, I expected everyone to be a straight shooter, but it turned out that more diplomacy was expected and my natural contrariness got me in some trouble. The most interesting workplace thing in France to me was that everyone shook hands with everyone every morning. So formal!

I'm getting to the point that some of my younger colleagues are a full generation younger than me. I had to explain what the Cold War was to someone recently, and who Keith Richards is. I find myself pedantically correcting people's grammar on e-mails. They scoff at me, but I think I'm doing them a favor. I'm always very formal with customers unless I've met them and made a personal connection. Younger people seem to assume informality from the get-go.

◀◀◀

Why Not?

Check out exciting options for learning like One Day University, in which you get to experience the joy of drinking in knowledge like when you were in college; your commitment to it is only one day. Of course you have one day!

If you don't have money, if you can't travel to a school, if you don't have time to sit in a classroom…sorry, none of these can be your excuses any more. Based on your own set of skills, strengths, and weaknesses, you can decide what it is that you want to do and you can find resources that are available.

Do you have to take classes that are directly connected to your current work? Take them only if your employer offers tuition assistance—and even then, there can be flexibility.

Yes, I'm a huge believer in continuing education, but how do you know what questions to ask? What if you don't know the questions to ask? You go to a teacher to learn something, but what do you do if you don't know what you need to learn? How do you know what you need? How do you figure out what classes to take?

▶▶▶

Words From the Wise—Phil Hall
Preeminent Vocal Coach and Voice Teacher for Musical Theater

Learning

When I was in college and graduate school, I never learned to sing correctly. I studied privately in New York City and, with the instruction and patience of one teacher, finally learned to keep my larynx down—the missing ingredient to my own voice. I was eternally grateful that I acquired that wisdom and ability. My acquired patience with my own pursuit helped me have infinite patience with the journeys of my own students.

I believe preparing the voice for theater auditions is more of a process and not a quick fix. Slow, steady, and methodical win the race. Learning to sing is really a scientific process that takes discipline and dedication. You can't really just add water and sing. I think singers do the best when they embrace their type and sing into it. The most frequent way singers derail is to be unprepared for auditions when they come along. Many try to learn brand new material for a specific audition because they feel they have nothing appropriate in their audition books. Often, nerves will kick in and they'll forget lyrics during the audition because they've not had enough living time with the lyrics to have fully inculcated them. When I can get singers to slow down, and to be thoughtful and methodical about their goals and how to achieve them, I find that they have a tendency to get back on track and have a greater chance of achieving their goals in what is still a business defined largely by subjectivity.

◀◀◀

SPARC-ing Knowledge

You should have someone who understands the importance of education in your network. It doesn't have to be a teacher, but it should be someone who's had some experience navigating a course catalog. Who's going to be the best at guiding you on your path? Someone who's had the same direct experience? Someone who's in the same field? Maybe that person is not specifically skilled in the area you're looking to develop in, but they can help you navigate your way there.

- ▶ Strategize: What's the game plan here? How much education are you seeking? How much time do you have to devote to it? Have your SPARC buddy hash this out with you.

- ▶ Purpose: What do you want to achieve from getting more educated? A new career? A richer life experience? Nurturing your avocation? Again, have your SPARC buddy ask the tough questions.

- ▶ Analyze: What are the best classes for you to take? Online or in person? Regular classes or one-off seminars? What's going to make the most sense for you?

- ▶ Rehearse: Your SPARC buddy can help you decide who you are and why you're at the class for the "go around" introductions. What will you say? They can help you devise that elevator pitch you need to describe yourself.

- ▶ Commit: Once you've decided on your plan, check in regularly with your SPARC buddy and let him or her in on your progress. Be open to the feedback your buddy provides. If he or she feels you're not committed enough, hear them out!

Remember, don't get defensive with your SPARC buddy. You want their honesty. You want them to stay on top of you.

Once you know what you need to do, you have to take action. You can't say, "Okay, I want to get more education in X" and not have a timeline in which you're going to accomplish it. You have to create a timeline for all of this, a schedule. If you don't, it will never happen.

Lastly, whatever these educational goals are that you have in place now, be sure to always have goals beyond those goals. Just like when you were in school, and extracurricular activities were important to supplement your classes, you need to have them now, too. Maybe it's the arts; maybe it's sports. Whatever it is, you need to expand your universe beyond your job skills. Find out what inspires you.

▶▶

Words From the Wise—Ron Raines
Musical Theater, Opera, Cabaret, Classical Music,
and Television Actor/Singer

Know Your Skills and Keep Improving

I continue to work on my voice and stay disciplined. My voice is my ticket to the future...wherever that may be. The phone keeps ringing, and for that I'm grateful. Actors have to reinvent, but people often begin reinventing before they've ever invented. Each of us has to start from where we are now, who we are now, and what we are now. We must find our center and determine what we're about as a person and as an artist before we begin to shape and embellish.

◀◀

Inspiration and Imagination

One of the greatest crimes of your life is to go through it uninspired. It's so important to make time in your schedule for creative or strategic thinking. Remember how we discussed in Chapter 4 about taking the first few moments of the day and letting your mind wander, and earlier in this chapter, when I suggested you learn more about the first thought you think about every day? You have to do this kind of thinking. You have to explore your world and daydream. You have to nurture your imagination by sometimes letting it do its thing. A much overlooked asset in the work environment from my experience is imagination. Not only is it not encouraged, it's devalued.

A friend of mine shared an e-mail with me that she received from her daughter's first-grade teacher. The teacher was annoyed at the child and wrote to the mother, something to the effect of "We all enjoy your daughter's imagination but not when she makes things up..."

Huh? What does this teacher, this shaper of young, six-year-old minds, think imagination is? That's scary. Imagination is devalued and it starts early.

When I am coaching a spokesperson for a keynote speech at a major conference, I'm constantly surprised at how scared they are to play, to make it fun to find ways to captivate their audience, to bring in their own uniqueness. It doesn't matter if they're Millennials or Boomers; somehow everyone's scared to play. Yet when they flex their creative juices, that's when they get ovations and high marks.

Also, there are major companies, Google being one, that look at potential employees for their ability to imagine, the Dare to be Great attitude, before even looking at which Ivy League school the candidate graduated from. One news item I read reported that Google isn't even interested in your college degree; they want to know what's deep down inside of you.

Bottom Line

Think of education as nourishment for success. You really can't get by without it. You need to keep curious and educate yourself daily. The more you know, the more you grow.

9

Ambition

Intelligence without ambition is a bird without wings.
—Salvador Dali

It doesn't matter how smart, educated, and focused you are and how well-planned your strategy; without ambition, you have no "fuel" to take you from self-sabotage to self-satisfaction.

Ambition is inherent in everyone. Sometimes it's stronger in some people. Why? Are some people naturally more ambitious than others? That's true in part, but there's more to it than that, especially where self-sabotage creeps in.

We sabotage our ambition when the planning we've done doesn't quite yield the results we wanted. Maybe you took a risk somewhere down the road and things did not turn out how you'd have hoped. You feel discouraged because you wanted things to go a certain way, and they didn't, and that makes you feel like you've failed. The sense of failure cripples, even paralyzes you, and you feel like maybe it's just better to stay with the status quo than to put all that work into putting yourself out there again to possibly fail again.

A colleague of mine, a brilliant journalist, has grieved for the past 30 years over not taking a job he had been offered way back when. He's let his whole life be poisoned by that one misstep. You can't let one misstep define you, no matter how big that misstep seems. You have to move on.

Maybe you feel that only "lucky" people get ahead. Yes, in every success story there is an element of luck, but I refer to it as "strategic luck." It's an instinct to seize the moment and act. It sounds cliché to say "you make your own luck," but it's true. Making your own luck is what advances you. Seize the moment. For example, my friend, Brad, short on funds but long on ambition, started an escort service to help fund his tuition to medical school. What's especially intriguing about this story is his sense of humor about his temporary occupation. In addition to his roster of clients, he has a button on his Website asking for donations to his medical school fund. And people, random people, donate. Now *that's* thinking out of the box.

Sometimes we allow our ambition to get shut down by others. Maybe you've wanted to do more to advance yourself and your career, but someone, or several someones, has been overly critical of you. Or maybe their complacency is rubbing off on you. (Remember the story of how Jane affected Martha's advancement in her career earlier in this book?)

Again, successful people understand that there will be bumps in the road. They know that these bumps exist either as unplanned outcomes or as people trying to sabotage their journeys. But they realize that when you're on a road to somewhere, you don't give up and go home when you make a wrong turn; you re-plot your course. They realize that a police officer or construction vehicle or accident ahead means a detour may be needed. They pull over, take a breath, and look at a map (or ask Siri for help).

Whatever the case, if your ambition is lying dormant, you're not going to get anywhere. You're like a car without gas. Let's get you re-fueled so you can take back the driver's seat when it comes to accomplishing your goals.

Killing It

A career skills class was being offered at no charge by my client's union, and she and I both thought it might be a worthwhile use of time and of Rose's limited financial resources to see if it could help spark some ideas about her future. This was a step in the right direction, for sure.

Except when we got together after the class, she didn't seem fired up and ready to conquer the world. Instead, she felt confused, and even a bit stunted. She brought with her the video of the skills session and we watched it together. I saw right away that this was a classic case of someone else shutting down ambition in others.

The instructor, a career coach donating his time, looked like a hobo; he was unshaven, unkempt and in over his head working with the level of professionals in the class. In watching the video, I realized he did not give

Rose even a shred of positive feedback. He was resolute in offering whatever negative feedback he could muster up in his lackluster way, but he offered nothing to instill confidence in Rose. He was condescending, self-important, and, as my friend from North Carolina loves to say, "Trying to make his own mess look big." As a result, Rose admitted, about halfway through the class, she shut down to protect what little shred of remaining dignity and self-respect she possessed.

I saw there was a lot of damage that had to be undone, and I explained to Rose that instead of shutting down, she needed to shut out everything she had learned in that class—that his teaching of this class had nothing to do with helping the students, it had to do with making this small person feel better about himself by belittling others. I also bet that the reason he was trying to knock down the student body was that he wanted their business in order to build them up again. A week later, Rose called me to tell me I was right. The instructor reached out on Facebook to befriend the students and began sending e-mails about his services. For him, it had been all about building a client base, and to do so, he had shut down the ambition of my client and so many others in the class.

This is a fairly blatant example of how someone can shut down ambition in someone else. But what about those times when it's not quite so obvious? What about the subtle ways people try to sabotage you? Remember when we discussed toxic people, how they will try to do what they can to throw you off course?

Anytime you feel like your plan has gone off course, fight against shutting it down. Take a "time out" and analyze what may have gone wrong. Ask yourself, "Is it really me that's stopping this from happening, or is it someone else?"

If you get a bad review, for example, whether by your supervisor at work, or for a performance or project you have out in the world, it doesn't mean you throw in the towel and give up on what you're doing forever. Before you give up on your strategy, before you decide to give up on your dream, sit down with your SPARC buddy and work it out.

▶▶

Words From the Wise—Phil Hall
Preeminent Vocal Coach and Voice Teacher for Musical Theater

It's What's Inside...

I facilitate goals and dreams. And I make people want to do their best. If students are passionate about something, I try to get them to think entrepreneurially—to think about what kind of entertainment they might present that they would be good at, and about which they are passionate. I encourage people to take risks on behalf of something they love.

I feel it's important to get still enough that you listen to your own voice inside of you. I think Barbra Streisand is a great example of a person who did that, and look what it got her. Oprah Winfrey is probably the second greatest example of a person who did that. Both of them knew what they should do and set themselves to the task of doing it. And look at what they created for themselves. I also respect Broadway star Patti LuPone for staying true to her vision, and tennis-pro sisters Venus and Serena Williams who had to fight for everything they have. Look at what they've accomplished already in their young lives.

◀◀

Getting That Spark Back...With SPARC!

Rose's instructor was in dire need of his own SPARC buddy, someone who could advise him that a good way to find new clients is not to go out and massacre people in order to save them. Can you imagine a doctor making people sick in order to have people to treat? A good SPARC buddy would have encouraged him to offer the class, to try and do as much good and positive work as he could. That way, he wouldn't make a client of everyone in the class, but he would have been able to forge an honest connection with a handful of students, even one student.

Luckily, Rose does have a SPARC buddy whom she can bounce things off. After she saw me, she worked with that buddy to try and get her ambition back on track. If your ambition seems off-track, go to your SPARC buddy. Explain that something seems amiss, that you feel like you've lost your way and need help re-navigating your course.

▶▶

"Why Not?"—Martin Samual
Actor/Singer/Dancer

For as long as I can remember, I've wanted to be a performer. I still remember watching American television as a kid and telling myself, that's what I want to do! But how was I going to get there? Growing up in a French Canadian family, I couldn't speak a word of English. It seemed impossible to learn a whole new language, but if I didn't speak English, I couldn't realize my dream.

When I was 20 years old, I learned about a casting for a new show in Toronto for the summer; they were looking for singers and dancers, and I decided to try out. I was super-nervous because it was my first time auditioning, but I was also going to have to sing a song in English. I chose "Something's Coming" from *West Side Story*, a super-fast and wordy song, which was probably the hardest song I could have picked given my circumstances. I didn't know any better.

The dancing part of the audition was first. I didn't understand a word the choreographer was saying, but I learned by watching and somehow managed to get by. Then they invited some of the group of dancers to stay and sing, and I was one of them. At this point, I was even more nervous because I'd have to stand in front of the producer and casting director, and sing the song I had learned phonetically. I didn't know how I was going to pull that off.

It took everything out of me to stand there and sing in front of all those important people who would be deciding my future, but I did it, and quite well, I might add. They were pleased with my performance and started to speak to me as soon as I finished my last notes. I didn't understand them, so I took a deep breath and said: "Martin, Montreal, I don't speak English!"

They seemed both perplexed and amused at this, and then kindly took me aside and tried to explain to me that they wanted me to be part of their show for the next six months. That's how I learned English!

A few years later, feeling quite comfortable with English, I decided to re-live this experience. Off I went to Germany and learned an entire show phonetically. It was very difficult at first, but then I started to learn and appreciate the language. After spending a year in that show, I decided to audition for a second show while I was in Germany. That's when I landed my first big leading role in German. Do you see a pattern here? A few years later, I moved to Miami where I started to learn Spanish and ended up doing a few Spanish soaps as well as other appearances in Spanish.

For someone who thought he couldn't learn other languages, I'm doing pretty well. I was afraid of how stupid I might sound learning a new language and all the work it would take, but I learned that with patience, hard work, and perseverance we can accomplish almost anything we want.

I am now an American citizen and live in New York City, the land of show business, and every day I ask myself, "What can I learn next? Maybe another language...."

◀◀

Being a Good SPARC Buddy

To have good SPARC buddies, you need to be a good one yourself. Remember, sometimes you'll need your SPARC buddy, and sometimes he or she needs you. Here are some important tips for being a good SPARC buddy:

1. Listen. When your SPARC buddy has the floor, it's about them, not you. Don't talk over them. Hear him or her out, wait till he or she is finished speaking, then you weigh in.

2. Have ideas. You know that your buddy is looking for advice, and you know this person well enough to know where they could use some guidance. Suggest ideas, but don't be insistent. Remember, this is not about you; it's about your buddy.

3. Be patient. Let your buddy vent and continue to try and pull information out of them even when it seems like they're done talking. Use phrases like "Is there anything else?" or "What more about this particular situation would satisfy you?" Don't worry, most people run out of steam in 20 minutes!

Taking It on Yourself

Your SPARC buddy can help you find that spark you need to get back your mojo, but you can also help yourself. It's all about getting in touch with your inner voice and taking your emotional temperature.

A great way to do this is to free associate a few minutes every morning before you hop out of bed to start the day. Set your alarm clock for 10 minutes earlier than usual to allow yourself time think. Try not to stress about all you have to do over the course of the day. Rather, just let your mind wander and don't try to rein in your thoughts to make them more productive. Giving yourself time to let your mind wander like this is actually productive on another level; it's helping you to see "bigger."

A very wise person once told me never keep running from task to task without taking a break. That's just what this is. It's a break we take before the insanity of our lives descends upon us. It's time we take to be alone with our thoughts and really figure out the big picture.

Sometimes we avoid being alone with our own thoughts and feelings because we're afraid. If we allow ourselves to explore too deeply, we might not like what we find. We have to get over that. Being able to see this big picture beyond the daily grind fuels our ambition. If we can't see it, we can't achieve it.

When to Say "When"

Another way we sabotage our ambition is by caving in and not staying true to our convictions. We let how others might feel about our actions influence us, and we don't act in our own best interest.

I had a friend several years back, let's call him Jack, who was trying to organize a charitable event for his company team. It was an ambitious endeavor that was sure not only to impress his superiors and earn him respect in the firm—for going that extra mile to give the company a worldwide presence—but would also feed his soul.

Unfortunately, Jack began to see that not everyone on his team was as committed to the endeavor as he was. In fact, it didn't seem like anyone else on his company's team was taking it seriously. Many members of the team blew off meetings, feeling like they were "donating" their time and talent, and that any other commitment was more important than this one.

Jack was getting frustrated at the situation and he complained to me. He asked me as a favor to come to his office and speak to the team, to help him get the message across that this event was important and he needed everyone's commitment to pull it off.

Being from the corporate sector and having facilitated thousands of meetings, I spun into corporate mode. I ran the meeting by the book (actually by my book, *Loud & Clear*), thinking I would be addressing a room of rational, linear thinking, highly functioning humans. That did not end up being the case.

Not only were they not taking the situation seriously, I also lost Jack's support. Here I was trying to help him motivate his own people, and he threw me under the bus by not standing up to them when they disagreed with me. Jack ended up having to cancel the event and I ended up with one less friend.

When you know you are not right for a project, a company, or a friendship, get out before the situation gets out of control. Winners never quit—except when it makes sense to quit. As soon as Jack saw he wasn't going to have the support of other members of his team, he should have either tried to replace the "dead weight," canceled the project early on, or even postponed it until he could assemble a better team and have more time to plan. This would have earned him way more respect than having a project with his mark all over it implode as it did.

Here's another example. I have a colleague, let's call her Laura, who runs a small consultancy. She recently took on two projects for a new client because she needed the money. However, neither project was a good match and she couldn't connect with the client. In fact, the client was impossible to work with, and she had felt right away that this was going to be the case. She ended up doing more work than agreed upon for what was starting to seem like less and less money, and so resentment built and festered. After a particularly volatile encounter, she exploded on the client and lost both projects. The lost work was an issue, but worse was that the situation compromised her reputation. At the very first indication of trouble she should have either bailed or had a sit down to manage expectations, but she didn't. She retreated to the corner with her tail between her legs, and let the situation roll over her.

▶▶

"Why Not?"—Riley Nelson
Student/Investor

You can secure your future in an uncertain economy. You're never too young to start. The only people who strike it rich in a gold rush are the ones who get there before it's a gold rush. I've been lucky enough this early in my life to be curious about finding such a thing, and, as a result, have made thousands of dollars thanks to Bitcoin, which I bought into when it was at only $8. At the time of this writing, 1 BTC (bitcoin) is worth $635, and I've been able to make even more through investments in this technology. I'm now looking for another investment within this niche. That's all my kind of success is about, hustling to find another niche that hasn't been found, or at least one that hasn't yet been fully explored.

There are enough possible "gold mines" for anyone to find, provided one keeps curious. That's not to say I haven't had some failures. I have made some bad investments. But personal investment capital doesn't have to be on the line to become successful; there are plenty of other routes.

I enjoy investing. There is no need to fear failure, because I'm really enjoying the process of doing it. The most important thing, I think, is that we need to remember why we do the things we do, and, even more importantly, we need to focus on how much enjoyment we get from things, even if they don't always end in "success." If your goal is to make money, or just "to be successful," without knowing exactly what you want that success in, and with your reason being that you want "to be happy," you're never going to be happy. Without passion and enjoyment, there isn't any point.

◀◀

Standing Tall

How often do we find ourselves not going after what we want or feel we deserved because we are afraid of losing a job or a client—or a lover? We can't do that, not anymore. We need to stand on our own two feet and learn how to deliver our demands in a way that isn't off-putting; in a way that makes others want to accommodate us.

Take your job, for example. Your bosses expect you to meet deadlines. It's not your boss's problem that your babysitter flaked out on you, your car broke down, or your in-laws are flying in for a month's stay. It's not about your needs; it's about your value. You need a team in place for your personal life; a network to call upon for help. And you need to cultivate healthy communication with your boss and your HR manager.

Give "Luck" a Chance

Do you believe only "lucky" people get ahead? Luck isn't about being blessed by the gods. It's about seeing an opportunity for all it can be, and jumping on it if it makes sense to do so. You have to jump when the opportunity is there. You may have to manufacture energy to seize it. You have to take risks.

Say, for example, that you're presented with a deadline. Some people may look at the deadline and decide no way is it possible that they can meet it, so they walk away from the opportunity. I'm not that way. When I'm faced with what looks like an impossible situation, I say "Yes" and then figure out how I'm going to get it done.

Ask yourself:

▶ What needs to be done?

▶ What training (if any) is required to get the job done?

▶ What resources are needed?

▶ What are the component parts of this task and what smaller deadlines can be established for them?

It's important to strive beyond the goal. Don't only take on projects you know will be easy because it feels comfortable to do so.

And know that when you push beyond what you think you can do, there's a chance you're going to fail. Good. I've already told you how I feel about failure. Don't let a disappointment kill you. You have to get beyond it. Every successful person I've ever met has taken luck by the throat, by taking whatever luck is offering them, and taking risks. If you never take a risk, you'll never get anywhere.

▶▶▶

"Why Not?"—Bud Martin
Executive Director, Delaware Theatre Company

All my life, all I ever wanted to do was direct. It wasn't a direct route.

I started teaching high school English and theater while I went to grad school. After I got my Masters in theater, I moved to a different school where I just taught and ran a theater program. I really wanted to direct professionally and I couldn't do that with a teaching schedule, so I quit teaching so that I could direct. I was working all the time and making about half as much money as I made teaching. My kids were getting a little thin and I realized that, for me to do the shows I really wanted to do, I had to finance them.

A guy that ran a small corporate finance consulting firm gave me a project for which they were not having a lot of success, to capitalize the Philadelphia USFL franchise. He said if I could turn that around, then I could have a job, so I started trying to figure out how to do that.

In the early 1980s, Philadelphia was a hot bed of high-tech companies that had just gone public. So I went through all the IPOs (initial public offerings), looked for overnight millionaires, and pitched them all on being part of "an expensive men's club." I built a very good book of wealthy people who enjoyed going to football games and I pitched them, "Here's your chance to indulge in a fantasy and own a football team."

I raised so much money that the company actually started a small brokerage division for me to run. I raised money for a lot of early stage companies and then a couple of us decided to leave that company and start our own.

I ended up forming my own investment banking firm in 1984, which I ran with my two partners for about five years. I started the first for-profit company that developed retirement communities and took it public. It was one of *Inc.* magazine's fastest growing public companies for two years in a row.

After that, I started three other companies that I took public and we enjoyed a lot of success, but my theater dream stayed alive. When my last company got acquired in 2008, I took over for Act II Play House's artistic director. The theater was struggling, he was stepping down, and I thought, well the timing might just work out. It meant cutting a lot of staff and costs and doing a lot of reprogramming of the seasons so that there were more attractive titles. During that time, I also produced five shows on Broadway and three in London.

I turned Act II around, and within a couple of years, I decided to freelance and produce more in New York. Then I got the call from Delaware Theatre Company. They were on the verge of closing and wondered if I would consider coming in to save the theatre.

In my first year, we doubled ticket sales. This year, my second, we doubled contributions. The Delaware Theatre Company is a great platform for me because it was a much bigger theater with a bigger budget and market than Act II Play House. I could actually fund things that I wanted to start with the hope of moving on to a longer life.

I feel that my experience has been unique, and I get asked to get involved in a lot of Broadway shows as a result because I'm not just somebody that can only raise money or invest. I actually know what I'm doing. A lot of producers that are really good producers are strong in one area; either they are strong at play development while relying on other people to raise money, or they're good at raising money and then they hire a really good team to pull off the show. I feel that my experiences enable me to have a foot in both camps. I feel pretty lucky to have had the experiences I did.

To keep art going in this world, we've got to be more business-like about it. That might seem horrendous, to certain people but you're seeing more art organizations fold because they didn't know how to manage their business. I'm fortunate to be able to do both.

◀◀

Bottom Line

Ambition is something you need to nurture to keep yourself relevant and on the right track. Although it's something that can get knocked out of us by negative people and those who don't want to see us succeed, we need to work to keep it fueled if we want to achieve success.

10

Faith

Faith is taking the first step, even when you don't see the whole staircase.
—Martin Luther King, Jr.

A lot of people don't quite understand what faith is and just how big it is. Many think faith has to do with religion and that if you have faith in your life's plan, that means you go to church or mass or temple or wherever regularly and you pray to God or Jesus or Allah.

But faith is much bigger than that. Faith is belief. Faith is what makes you know that even without immediate proof, the choices you've made and the course you're on are the right ones. And that's bigger than anything that will ever happen in any church.

Why does faith matter in a book about fighting self-sabotage? It's because faith is what pulls all your efforts together. It's the glue for all these pieces that may seem disconnected that are meant to come together to make you your best you. It's what makes you know that even if you're taking a risk by switching jobs or careers, then everything's going to work out fine.

Faith is more than this, though. In a world that seems designed to cripple you, in which so many things work against you, faith is also taking the time to feed your soul. You need to make time for you, to energize and revitalize.

▶▶

Words From the Wise—Ron Raines
Musical Theater, Opera, Cabaret, Classical Music,
and Television Actor/Singer

Passion First

Art feeds my soul and the souls of all artists who have survived within the human element of that concept. Unfortunately, art has nothing to do with survival in the business.

The business of art is a whole other thing. Art is the beauty and the soul that touches you. To survive the business of art and make a living at it is the hardest thing in the world. I recently was telling a young singer that my wife and I have made a life doing what we love to do. We're not superstars and that's not what we wanted to be. We do what we do because we are passionate about doing it. Our passion has always been music, singing, acting, and for my wife, Dona, also directing. That's it. I challenge Dona, and Dona challenges me. We don't let one another get away with B.S. We call each other on it every time. She's my buddy. We're very grateful to have made a life for ourselves and yet, we worked our butts off! Now we continue our paths by teaching others what we have spent a lifetime learning.

◀◀

Anton, Adrift

It always amazes me when I encounter clients who, on paper, should be superstars. They have all the right education and training, yet their career track record doesn't seem to reflect any of it.

Take Anton, for example, a client I recently coached. A good-looking, seemingly well-put-together lawyer, he had two Ivy League degrees. At age 45, though, he was still an associate at a firm when his education and years of service should have made him a partner, an associate partner or, at the very least, a senior associate at this point in his career. People who had joined the firm later than him were already blazing the partner trail, yet Anton stagnated. He wanted to get ahead. He tried to dress well. He tried doing different things to get noticed, like giving presentations to the partners, but nothing was happening for him.

His supervisors noted in reviews that his work was fine, that he was a nice guy who got along well enough with others and who didn't court controversy or cause conflicts. In fact, it wasn't Anton who had sought out my services at all, but his managing partner, Isabella. She was on his side and felt a little training might make him a better presenter and, thus, help him to impress the big wigs who signed off on promotions.

Let's take a step back. Anton had:

▶ Attitude—He was a team player, not poison or toxic to be around.

▶ Aptitude—He had every single degree necessary, plus extra coursework.

▶ Appearance—He was well-groomed and well-dressed.

▶ Focus—He did his work; he didn't miss deadlines.

▶ Ambition—He really wanted to get ahead.

▶ Image—There were no "red alerts" in his social media; he used every platform correctly and with professionalism.

I knew all of this from speaking to Isabella, looking at his file, and Googling him. It was a mystery to me why he wasn't getting ahead. Then I met Anton and I spent about half an hour speaking with him. That's when I realized what was amiss.

Anton had no *faith* in his ability, no passion. He wanted to get ahead, sure, but when I asked him questions about how things would change for him, how his role in the firm would be different, how his new position would impact his personal life and his family, he had nothing to say. It was as if getting ahead was a program entered into his "database"; he had no emotional connection to the prospect of getting to his goal.

I began to realize this meant he really didn't believe he could get to his goal; he was just going through the motions of what had been ingrained in him and what was expected of him. That's why he wasn't succeeding.

If you don't believe in your heart and soul that you're going to get something, you're not going to get it. You need that faith, that belief, or you're wasting your time.

Here's the issue, though. The trouble is, we're all so consumed by the mechanics of getting to "there," we don't take the time to think, or, more accurately, to feel it through. We spend all our time jumping through hoops and not enough time feeding our souls. Having a soul that's nourished and fortified helps you have faith.

▶▶▶

Words From the Wise—Jeff Winton
Senior Vice President/Chief Communications Officer
for Astellas Pharma

Feeding Your Soul

I have been blessed with a very full and robust life. Much of my personal life centers around my partner of 26 years, my family, and my dogs, cattle, and horses. My partner, Jim, and I have been breeding and competing with our champion Whippets and Greyhounds for more than 20 years. We own a commercial dairy farm in New York where we have more than 200 head of registered dairy cattle who live a life better than most people. A few years back, we spent more than $50,000 and bought them all new mattresses. People who think animal agriculture is inhumane have not met our "girls."

One of the rewards of this full life is that we move in so many different circles and have the most diverse set of friends that you would ever imagine, ranging from CEOs of major corporations to farm workers who milk our cows for us. When we throw a party, you would be really surprised by what a tapestry of humanity is assembled. I was taught at an early age to treat everyone the same. My father was a farmer and a school bus driver and so, as a young boy, I understood that a bus driver was as important, if not more so, than the high school principal. As a result, even to this day, I talk with our cafeteria workers and cleaning people at my company as much as I do with the senior management.

My animals feed my soul certainly, as does running and exercising. I am probably one of the few people who actually prefers to run on my own and not with other people because it is my time to think and clear my mind without talking with others. Religion and spirituality are also very important to me, and that certainly feeds my soul. I rarely watch television so when I do have down time at home, I like to sit in silence, think, and reflect. Silent contemplation is definitely underrated.

◄◄

How Do You Feed Your Soul?

What does your soul need to survive? Everyone is different. Maybe you need an hour of quiet to yourself in a day, a space in which you can clear your head, meditate, and focus. Maybe you need to do something active several times a week, something good for your body that makes you feel alive and complete.

Perhaps you need to make more time for your family. In an April 14, 2014 *Huffington Post* piece, performer Melissa Errico stated, "Not only do I have an obligation to myself to re-group, but I have an obligation to [my family]. It's really important to have a different rhythm outside of the ebbs and lows of the profession. In my case, it's a family tribe. We're a soul tribe, and there's so much affection and passion."

Earlier in this book, we talked about giving yourself time to breathe; about meditating and really thinking about what you want out of life instead of just obsessing with what happens to be going on in your life. We talked about re-training your brain in the way you think about things.

Says Jeff Winton, "In my current job, I am traveling a great deal as our headquarters is based in Tokyo. But I love long flights as it is the only opportunity I get in my busy life to disconnect from the outside world while having a glass of wine or two and watching multiple movies. I'm always sad after a long flight is over and I am forced to enter back into the chaotic world again!"

What fuels you? What grounds you? What supports you? How do you feed your soul?

It's time to take out that journal again. I want to you to find a fresh page and, on a left-hand-side page, and at the top, I want you to write "10 Things I Wish I Had More Time to Do Daily." On the opposite page, I want you to write "10 Things I Have to Do Daily and Don't Want to Do."

Take your time with both the "Want To" and the "Don't Want To" columns. It's easy enough to fill the "Want To" column with things like "exercise" or "eat better" or "get a manicure," but I want you to dig more deeply than that. Why do you want to make time to exercise daily? How would getting a manicure fulfill you?

Do the same with the other side. It's easy enough to fill the column of things you don't want to do with "laundry," "driving to work," and "grocery shopping," but I want you to try and dig deeper than that—for both columns. Don't just write the first thing that pops into your mind that you don't want to be doing.

Think it through. Figure out why you don't want to do that particular thing. When you get to the heart of why you want to and don't want to do things, you'll get a better sense of what you want out of life and why.

Finding Your Core

Although it's easy to believe that other people will help you, you can't rely on that. You can't rely on other people to make you feel exceptional, throwing praise and opportunities at you. You have to have that confidence in yourself, in your core. You can't rely on others to instill confidence in you; you'll never get anywhere that way.

To grow more confident, you might have to pull your confidence from someplace else. Where have your happy moments been? How have you shined? Even if you're not shining at your job right now, can you pull those moments somehow and draw from them? Remember: There's no business like show business and all business is "show." This is how actors get involved in their parts. They draw from their experiences to be able to show deep sadness and sorrow and, also, great joy. What can you draw from in your own experience that can help you "act the part" and get what you want?

▶▶

Words From the Wise—Phil Hall
Preeminent Vocal Coach and Voice Teacher for Musical Theater

What's At Your Core

I'm incredibly lucky that I make a living in music. When I was a child, I was very shy and my hands shook (I think it was because I was nervous that I was what turned out to be gay), and my parents read an article that piano playing was good therapy for nervous children. That led my father to find this deliciously eccentric and extraordinarily accomplished piano teacher named Alice Camden Hundley in Durham, North Carolina. She was the very best thing that could have ever happened to me at that point in my life. She gave me music theory, four-part dictation, voice-leading, and piano lessons for a number of years. When she wanted me to play something in a certain way, she played it on the inside of my arm with her own fingers so I could feel how she wanted me to "voice" the notes as I played them. She was a gift in every way imaginable. Because of her, I learned to play by ear; I did well in theory in undergraduate school, and taught ear-training, sight singing, and theory to freshman to pay my way through graduate school, and was even sought out during testing for admission to graduate school at Juilliard to be a theory major there.

There has never been a single moment that music has ever let me down, or has disappointed me. There has never been a single time I've not come away enriched by whatever time I've been able to spend on music either by myself, with a group, or with my students. Music has been my mistress, my lover, and has always given, given, given without demanding anything in return. So rich is the reward I get from giving music its due, that I simply can't do it any other way. It's a dilemma I'm grateful to have.

◀◀

Take a Timeout

Take a timeout not as a punishment but as a gift to yourself. If you lost your job, for example, you may feel like if you're not spending every minute finding a new one that you're wasting your time. That's just not the case. You need to take time for yourself to savor the small things. Step out of the havoc of your life and...

- ► Take a nap.
- ► Stream a few episodes of a show you've been meaning to watch.
- ► Take a walk.
- ► Have a good laugh; it's a mini vacation for you and everyone around you.
- ► Have sex.

Note especially that last one. When you're feeling stuck, your sex drive seems somewhere far away, but you have to work to get it back. Remember earlier when we talked about smiling, that if you make yourself smile enough, you'll just start to smile naturally? The same goes for sex. Sometimes just allowing yourself to do it will make you want to do it.

Because here's the thing: Self-sabotage is a terrible thing for you and your partner. While you're working on yourself, remember that it isn't just about *you* if you have a partner; it's about the both of you.

If ever there was a time in our history when we needed "date night" it's now. The germ of self-sabotage, in my experience, can start when we close down and feel there is no room for a night out, an afternoon out, a morning break with our partner or best friend. One day a week for two hours is enormously restorative and saves partnerships.

You need to get perspective, especially if you're a parent of young kids. Share babysitting with your SPARC buddy so that you can step out with your partner for a few hour fling. Otherwise what ends up happening is that your pillow talk becomes about who is taking baby Alice to the playgroup the following day, and not connecting as human beings in love. Make time to reconnect with your partner at least once a month. Don't talk about money struggles or issues involving your kids. Remember what you talked about when you first got together.

Start out once a month and work up to once a week—at least. Your relationship and your resilience will improve.

▶▶

Words From the Wise—Merri Sugarman
Casting Director, Tara Rubin Casting in New York

Give of Yourself

Not long after I'd moved to Los Angeles and had just begun my career in casting, still feeling a little lost and uprooted and desperately trying to feed my soul, I had a very vulnerable conversation with a friend. It was sort of a dark time for me emotionally and nothing was helping to pull me up and out of that place, not therapy or exercise or socializing or traveling—all the things that had proven helpful in the past.

But that changed after this pal suggested I try some volunteer work. She said, with love, "I know this sounds harsh but it might not be a bad idea to simply get out of your own head, remove the focus from yourself and do something strictly for someone else." She suggested Big Sisters.

And so I embarked on a journey that did more than just get me out of my own head. After an orientation and an extremely invasive intake process that took more than six months (which gave me a lot of time to back out on what I'd been repeatedly told would have to be a very real, long-term commitment—not my forte—and really forced me to look at some hard personal facts), I met Jenny. She was 7 years old. It was love at first sight. Now Jenny's almost 22—we've been through a lot. She's probably taught me more than I've taught her but I'll never tell her so! She reminds me every day that when things are bleak, if we stay open to things that are new—and maybe take us out of our comfort zones—the universe *will* provide.

◀◀

Pull Out of Yourself

It's easy when we're stuck to focus on our own misery. As we discussed earlier, we're human. It's okay to feel bad for yourself. It's okay to grieve. What isn't okay is to have that grief or despair or frustration swallow you. You have to pull out of yourself.

Merri Sugarman found a great way to pull out of her own bad time in life. Not only was she able to help herself recover, but she also became a mentor for a girl who may not have had any good role models in her young life. Merri got better because she had to rise to it—not only for herself but for the little girl who counted on her.

It's a wonderful thing that people are giving back to their community, especially with the rise of underemployed and unemployed people who are gravitating to volunteering to keep connected, feed their soul, and use their time effectively.

▶▶

"Why Not?"—Staff Sergeant Tom Blakey
Volunteer/National WWII Museum in New Orleans

I always wanted to be the best. That's why I became a paratrooper in the Army. Growing up, we were really poor. Mom was raising two boys alone. I always had the desire to own my own business, so I had a lot of drive. After the Army, I went to work in the oil business and eventually formed my own business. We had three headquarters—in New Orleans and Lafayette, Louisiana, and in Houston. I sold the business in 1975 and retired.

I now volunteer at the National WWII Museum, which tells the stories of the American experience in the war that changed the world so that all generations will understand the price of peace and be inspired by what they learn.

In telling young Americans about my WWII history, I hope I'm helping them to understand about the country they're from and how that history has and will affect their futures. In most cases, I get a sense of interest and curiosity and gratitude. It's certainly gratifying to me. I love showing a group of youngsters the clickers or "crickets" that they know only as toys, and telling them how they were an essential communication tool on D-Day, when paratroopers dropped behind enemy lines in the pre-dawn hours of the Normandy Invasion. It's a thrill to watch their eyes widen in wonder at the story of this real-life drama.

I wake up every day excited to go to the Museum. It inspires me—keeps me going. When I first became a volunteer, I signed on to be a docent for the Normandy exhibition galleries, because that's where I served. But I have become more and more impressed with the Museum through the years as it has grown and expanded, and more and more committed to it. What it is doing and teaching is so important. Somebody said I'm like a "walking mission statement" of the Museum! That's about the best thing I could be!

Mission Statement: The National WWII Museum tells the stories of the American experience in the war that changed the world—why it was fought, how it was won, and what it means today—so that all generations will understand the price of peace and be inspired by what they learn.

◄◄

Connect With Success

To achieve success, you have to "bridge" to it, and one of the most important bridges you need to build is your passion for having that success. If you don't feel passionate about the end-game, how do you honestly expect you're ever going to be able to stay in the game and put up with everything you need to get through to get there? Passion is the fuel of getting to success and passion comes directly from the soul.

Faith significantly comes into play here, too. Think about what passion is—it's an uncontrollable, sometimes irrational, urge to be doing something, something that fuels you. Nothing makes you "think" you should do something you feel passionate about. When the passion's there, what choice do you have? You do it, believing there's no other choice.

Passion is action infused with belief. Belief is the root of faith. Faith is essential to succeeding. Are you seeing how this is all tying together now? Good!

▶▶

"Why Not?"—Richard Berg
Board Game Designer

I always wanted to be in theater. I liked entertaining people, but my parents said, "law school," so instead of performing, I spent three years "studying" the law. In my last year, I put on a massive "Law Review Show" with a good friend who went on to have a Hollywood film career. Me, I became a lawyer.

I started off with the old Estate Tax Division of the IRS. "You die, we pry," was how I answered the phone, quickly learning how little sense of humor the IRS had. I left the IRS and went on to become a criminal defense trial attorney, which I couldn't figure out until I realized it was simply theater with a captive audience of 12. The actual law had little to do with what I did; it was mostly keeping the jury entertained so that they bought my points.

In the meantime, I had been engaging myself in another passion: board games, something I had been fascinated with since I was about 10. I started musing about whether I could actually design one on my own, not having the vaguest idea how. But one of the advantages of being a criminal defense lawyer was that you spent plenty of time sitting in a courtroom waiting, with nothing to do—more than plenty of time. So I started to design games—well, in note form—while waiting.

I began to design some historical simulation board games, finding it quite enjoyable, introspective, personal, and devoid of any of the tremendous baggage that being a defense attorney carried.

Soon I was doing more board game design and less practicing law. Instead of working regular hours, five days a week, driving to work in horrendous New York City traffic and having to do the daily Olympian task of finding a parking spot, as a board game designer, I was only responsible for myself, how I did what I did, and how serious I took my new profession. I've now been doing that for 20 years and I still wake up every day looking forward to doing more.

◀◀

Passion vs. Profession

So over the course of your exploration, you've learned that you're not passionate about graphic design at all but what really fuels you is cake decorating. However, you've spent $65,000 getting a degree in graphic design so you can start making money and you can't find any way (right now) that cake design is going to pay your mortgage.

Of course, it isn't always an option to just jump ship and switch careers. It's possible that all you really need in your life is a passion boost, a way to infuse your life with color.

▶▶

"Why Not?"—Linda Moshier
Singer, Gardener, Wife

In April of 2011, I stopped my life for six weeks. I closed up my New York City apartment, packed up the truck, and with my husband and two dogs, drove across the country to Flathead Lake, Montana, to study permaculture. At the end of that intensive, eye-opening, ultra-earthy six weeks, my husband and I put together a design for our own property. We worked on this design as a team, each bringing ideas and design elements we felt were important to the project. What had been our giant grass lawn suddenly became the underpinning of an edible food forest.

Probably the greatest joy of all is that my husband and I now have a collective dream, a common cause, and a lifelong project. We work separately and together on implementing the food forest and can share in each other's triumphs as we watch our dream slowly take shape.

Just the other day, while I was putting in another tomato patch, my husband looked at me and said, "I love you."

I smiled and asked, "Why?"

He replied, "Because you are so committed!"

Switching gears mid-life from consumer to homesteader, from shopper to gardener, and from traditional to adventurous has reinvigorated our lives and strengthened our relationship.

It has also helped us get through the failures that inevitably come along.

Who's to say why we choose to suddenly go in a different direction in our lives? Opportunities arise, circumstances change, disillusionment with the old or discovery of the new. Sometimes, in a moment, all of these things collide. You let go of the life you knew and embrace something completely outside yourself. You find that not only do you have the strength to get through all kinds of new challenges, but you feel doubly satisfied at the results because *you* made them happen. Go create something new together. Why not? What have you got to lose but a crop of gooseberries now and then?

◄◄◄

What Now?

Don't quit your job. That's okay. But make time for your passion. When you start to nurture it, to give it the attention it needs, the possibilities of what you can do will begin to grow. Your perspective will change. It won't happen overnight, it might take years. But if you devote yourself enough to your passion, it will take charge. As long as it takes charge in a way that doesn't leave you destitute, you'll be okay. And before it totally becomes your life's focus, just having it there will make your life more fulfilling.

Can you leave what you spent years of your life and thousands of dollars being trained to do? Maybe, maybe not. Remember: You are going to die. We are all going to die. Your time on this earth is limited. You want to spend it doing something that brings you joy and satisfaction.

Living a life without joy or satisfaction is the biggest self-sabotage of them all.

Bottom Line

When you started this journey with me, I told you that not everyone was going to get behind you, and I meant it. You're probably starting to see even now who's going to stick with you and who you're going to be better off without. The one person you're never going to be without, however, is yourself. That's really the bottom line of this chapter and of this whole book. If this is going to work, you need to have faith in yourself. You need to act on the other areas I've illustrated for you as we've gone through this journey away from self-sabotage together—but if you don't believe in your heart and soul that this is possible, it's never going to happen for you and you will continue to feel lost.

I don't want you ever to feel perpetually lost.

I want you to believe in *you*. I want you to imagine a world in which you have everyone's support in order to grow into the best possible you. I want you to believe that people are cheering you on, that strangers you meet want nothing more than for you to reach this goal.

Think of this like a run you take in the morning or evening, a work-out. When you get tired, I want you to try and push back against being tired. It's going to happen; you're going to get exhausted from all of this. But I want you to believe that you have strength beyond that point of exhaustion, that if you push just a little bit beyond it, all you're going to find is a new reserve of energy you didn't even know you had. You have your SPARC buddies; call on them to get you through.

You finished this book. You got to this point. See? The power to succeed is in you.

It's time to put the strategies you've learned here in action. It's time to fuel your dreams and ambition with the "Why Nots" of those who have taken this journey before you and made it.

Go ahead. Change your life.

You got this.

About the Contributors

Deborah McCarthy is director of Results Delivery Organization, Alcatel-Lucent. She has a BS in Engineering from Rutgers College of Engineering and an MBA in International Economics and Finance from Fairleigh Dickinson University. Her achievements include Bell Labs Entrepreneurial Boot Camp Winner for NetHead Telepresence Seed Venture, Bell Labs President's Award for Application Intelligent Network Platform, Primetime Engineering Emmy Award by the Academy of Television Arts and Sciences as a member of the Grand Alliance Digital TV Standard team from Bell Laboratories.

Julia Murney appeared on Broadway as Elphaba in *Wicked* after playing the role on the national tour for which she received an Acclaim Award, among other prominent stage roles. Her TV credits include *30 Rock, Sex and the City, Brothers and Sisters, Ed, NYPD Blue*, all three *Law and Orders*, and many voiceovers. A Syracuse University graduate, her recordings include the original cast albums of *The Wild Party* and *A Class Act*, the Grammy-nominated Actor's Fund Benefit of *Hair*, and her first solo album, *I'm Not Waiting*, available on Sh-K-Boom Records and at Juliamurney.com.

Kevin B. McGlynn is a graduate of the Boston Conservatory who has performed in 48 states, 13 countries, and on five continents in productions including *Kiss Me Kate, All Shook Up*, and *Forbidden Broadway*. His favorite regional roles include Jesus in *Jesus Christ Superstar*, Tom Andrews in *Titanic*, and Lumiere in *Beauty and the Beast*.

Cheryl A. Marshall, PsyD, is a clinical psychologist and published author who has helped people overcome self-sabotage through psychotherapy for more than 25 years.

Cathy Russell is an actress, teacher, and entrepreneur who's featured in the *Guinness Book of World Records* for the show *Perfect Crime*, which has been running since 1987 (she's missed only four performances in 28 years and performs eight shows a week). She's also general manager of the Snapple Theater Center in Times Square and co-director of the Sedgwick-Russell Acting Studio.

Gee Rittenhouse, PhD, is vice president and general manager of Cloud and Virtualization for Cisco. He has held many senior executive positions and is able to seamlessly balance visionary technical leadership with practical business insight. Dr. Rittenhouse is a highly respected thought leader who has appeared before the U.S. Congress, U.S. Federal Communications Commission, European Presidential Commission, and World Economic Forum. He has published numerous articles and holds over a dozen patents.

Rob Sedgwick is an actor, producer, and the scion of one of America's oldest and most notable families. His acting career has spanned 26 years and encompasses film, television, and the New York stage, where he has also produced several off-Broadway plays. Rob is co-director of the Sedgwick Russell Acting Studio in New York City and is working on his memoir, *Bob Goes to Jail*.

Sharon Halley is a choreographer for Broadway and off-Broadway productions, as well as the New York City Opera, television, and regional theater. She has also worked internationally in Germany and Brazil.

James Gerth is senior consultant for CommCore Strategies and associate director of Infinity Repertory Theatre Company. He has trained several thousand clients including executives, sales managers, scientists, physicians, and corporate communications managers in the art of message development and delivery. He has also performed on Broadway and in theaters around the world. He has been the commercial spokesman for Verizon, Marriott Hotels, GE Capital, Citibank, Radio City Music Hall, Madison Square Garden, and the United States Postal Service.

Robert Diamond is founder/CEO/editor-in-chief of BroadwayWorld.com, the largest theater Website in the world.

Karen Arlington is a stage and film actor and singer based in New York. She is a proud member of SAG-AFTRA and AEA.

Melissa Errico has starred in seven musicals including *My Fair Lady* and *White Christmas*, and has also released three solo CDs, most recently *Legrand Affair*. A Tony-nominated star who works regularly on television and film, she is in her 10th year as founder of a New York non-profit charity to support expectant and new mothers called the Bowery Babes. She's married to tennis star Patrick McEnroe and has three daughters.

Michael Mastro has worked professionally as an actor on stage and screen for more than 25 years, appearing on Broadway, in films, and in episodic television. During the last 10 years, he's added directing, teaching, and career coaching for actors to his repertoire. He lives in New York City.

Karl duHoffmann went from Broadway dancer to Spirits brand manager at Anchor Distillers. He is the founder of Orchard Hill Cider Mill.

Catherine Hickland played Lindsay Rappaport on *One Life to Live* for 11 years and Fantine on Broadway in *Les Miserables*. She is an entrepreneur, author, speaker, entertainer, and game changer.

Michael James Scott began his acting career at age 11 in Orlando, Florida. A Broadway favorite with eight Broadway shows, film, and television to his credit, he is also a teacher for young artists and prodigy of legendary performer Ben Vereen. Scott originated the role of "the Maggots Guy" in the Tony Award-winning *Book of Mormon* and as understudy has played the Genie in *Aladdin* on Broadway. He lives in New York.

Karla Visconti is director, Corporate Communications Caribbean and Latin America for Hilton Worldwide. Karla has more than a decade of experience in public relations and corporate communications, having spearheaded a number of promotional initiatives/campaigns, managed crisis communications, and supported corporate social responsibility efforts.

Laureen Cook is the principal TMT advisor, IFC (World Bank), for the Telecommunications, Media, and Technology investment sector. She has 25 years of worldwide telecommunications experience and has held Executive and BOD roles with leading telecommunications operators worldwide; MTC-Vodafone (ME), Deutsche Telekom (Germany), Cable & Wireless (UK), NYNEX (USA), Debitel (Germany), Telestet (Greece), and Satelindo (Indonesia). She holds an MSc in Telecommunications Engineering from Rochester Institute of Technology, and an MBA from Long Island University in New York.

Laurence Julliard has nearly 20 years of experience both in Europe and the U.S. managing strategic and tactical speakers, internal and external flagship events such as Mobile World Congress and Broadband World Forum, among others across telecommunications services. Laurence has a strong track record for delivering efficient go-to-market campaigns and demonstrating return on investment with large and complex corporate companies. She is currently a consultant leading the ICT (Internet Communication and Telecom) expertise within MCI Group, and runs a family pension in the French Alps. She lives with her husband and three children.

Lee Koenigsberg, MBA, ChFC, has been assisting people in developing plans for their long-range financial security for 30 years in a practice that provides superior service.

Cheryl Raymond is manager of Public Programs and Special Events, New York Public Library for the Performing Arts at Lincoln Center. She presents more than 150 free live programs yearly, including new Broadway musicals as works in progress, classical concerts, lectures, panel discussions, and concert versions of operas.

Karen Radwin is executive director of the American Cancer Society's Hope Lodge Program in New York and New Jersey. She has spent her professional career of 39 years in not-for-profit management, the last 30 of which have been with the American Cancer Society.

Merri Sugarman is a casting director with Tara Rubin Casting in New York. A former actor in such hits as *Les Miserables*, Merri now devotes her time to casting such Broadway hits as *Spamalot, Jersey Boys, The Phantom of the Opera*, and many others. She is also the proud casting director of the Web series *Submissions Only*. Prior to joining Tara Rubin Casting, Merri was director of casting for dramas and movies at ABC Television, overseeing the casting of *ALIAS, NYPD Blue*, and *The Practice*, to name a few.

Katherine M. Mastrota, MS, OD, FAAO, is center director of Omni Eye Surgery, New York and a Fellow of the American Academy of Optometry. She is a diplomate of the American Board of Optometry. Dr. Mastrota is contributing editor to *Contact Lens Spectrum* and the online newsletter, *Optometric Physician*. She sits on the editorial board of *Advanced Ocular Care, Refractive EyeCare*, and *Optometry Times* and has authored numerous articles for these as well as other professional publications. She is an advisor to a number of pharmaceutical companies. Dr. Mastrota was named secretary to the Ocular Surface Society of Optometry (OSSO) and the Anterior Segment Section of the American Academy of Optometry. She has lectured locally and nationally on ocular surface disease and other topics. Serving the profession, she is a past member of the board of directors of the Optometric Society of the City of New York.

Angelo Lambrou developed a love for fashion in his teenage years and studied fashion in Johannesburg and later London. Over the past 20 years, he has dressed private individuals for special occasions, designed uniforms, and created new and fresh images for large corporations. He is based in New York.

Alan Matarasso, MD, is a board-certified aesthetic plastic surgeon with a clinical practice in New York City. He is currently the vice president elect of Aesthetic and Private Practice for the American Society of Plastic Surgeons. Dr. Matarasso also achieved the part of clinical professor of plastic surgery at Albert Einstein College of Medicine and is involved in the training of plastic surgery fellows and residents at three plastic surgery residency programs in New York City. Dr. Matarasso has lectured at more than 400 national and international meetings and professional symposiums on aesthetic surgery. He is author of more than 250 peer-reviewed journal articles, monographs, and textbook chapters.

Lana Gersman has made up everyone who's anyone, including the last four American Presidents, Sting, Paul and Linda McCartney, and has been a personal makeup artist to the following show hosts: Tina Brown, Paula Zahn, Elizabeth Vargas, and Anderson Cooper, to name a few. Find her online at LanaGmakeup.com.

Dr. John Foreyt, PhD, is a professor in the Department of Medicine and the Department of Psychiatry and Behavioral Sciences, and director of the DeBakey Heart Center's Behavioral Medicine Research Center, Department of Medicine at Baylor College of Medicine in Houston, Texas. Dr. Foreyt is an international thought leader and has published extensively in the areas of diet modification, cardiovascular risk reduction, eating disorders, and obesity. He has published 17 books and more than 360 articles in these areas.

Ricardo Morales, ISSA, NASM, MAX30, VIPR, FMS, has this philosophy: if your mind can believe, the body can achieve. Ricardo is a certified personal fitness trainer at Equinox, which operates 66 upscale, full-service clubs in the U.S. as well as internationally. Equinox provides a holistic approach to fitness and offers an integrated selection of Equinox-branded programs, services, and products, and has developed a lifestyle brand that represents service, value, quality, expertise, innovation, attention to detail, market leadership, and results.

Scott Warren is a Life Style Designer who works to make daily living as happy, beautiful, and fulfilling as possible through design and environment.

Jeff Winton was born and raised on his family's dairy farm in the Chautauqua region of western New York State, and was the first person in his family to attend college. After having spent several years in the Agricultural Communications arena in advertising and public relations, he eventually moved into Human Health. He is currently senior vice president and chief communications officer for Astellas Pharma, a large global company based in Tokyo, and president of the Astellas Foundation in the U.S.

Jeremy Merrifield is creative director/cofounder of Jupiter Highway, a consortium of professionals from a cross section of disciplines, providing out-of-the-box brand messaging, storytelling content, and cinematic production. It was founded with a simple mission: make creative work.

C. Charles "Chuck" Pineda, PE/CGC/AVS, is president, managing director, Trans-Infra PPP, LLC. He is a professional engineer and certified general contractor with over 33 years of experience, including leadership roles on major rail transit and rail-related infrastructure projects. Mr. Pineda founded the New York firm of Trans-Infra PPP, LLC to provide consulting services to public and private sector clients interested in developing transportation infrastructure projects via the use of Public Private Partnerships and alternative project delivery.

John Frazier is executive vice president of Quinn, a New York lifestyle public relations agency with global impact. Quinn's disciplined, strategic approach has built some of the world's largest audiences. John's broad knowledge and expertise make him one of their most client-pleasing, award-winning professionals.

Andre Mechaly is marketing and strategy director of Network and Infrastructure Systems at Thales. He began his career as a software engineer, and upon discovering that though people could explain how a product works, few could explain what the products are used for, which led him to transition from R&D to Product Management and then to Product Marketing and Communications.

Douglas DeMarco is the executive producer and owner of Brown Paper Bag, Inc., a digital imaging studio specializing in the combining of new digital media including videography.

Richard Armstrong, MD, works for Horizon Family Medical. He spent the majority of his career at St Luke's-Cornwall Hospital in Newburgh, New York, an affiliate of Mount Sinai Hospital in New York City. There, he was attending anesthesiologist and director of the Pain Management and Palliative Care service.

Grant Herman is a cloud-based solutions analyst at Booz Allen Hamilton, a leading provider of management and technology consulting services to the U.S. government in defense, intelligence, and civil markets. He has supported global banks as a war game analyst and as lead regulatory compliance reviewer, and also assisted as a software developer and tester.

Samantha Stroh Bailey is a professional editor, published author, and journalist, who owns Perfect Pen Communications. Her work has appeared in *Now Magazine, The Village Post, Oxford University Press, Abilities Magazine, Kobo Writing Life*, and many other publications, and she was one of Kobo Writing Life's writers-in-residence at Book Expo America 2013. Samantha also has a Master of Education in Applied Linguistics. The author of *Finding Lucas*, Samantha is also co-editor of the fiction anthology *A Kind of Mad Courage*. She lives in Toronto with her husband and two children.

Art Stevens is managing partner of StevensGouldPincus. Art also co-founded LobsenzStevens, one of the top 25 independent public relations firms, and ran it for more than 25 years before it was acquired by Publicis Group in 1999. The recipient of a number of Lifetime Achievement Awards, he is also author of *The Persuasion Explosion*, a behind-the-scenes look at the role of public relations in everyday life.

Phong Vu is partner of the Consumer Driven 6-Sigma Management Institute, a data-driven methodology that uses statistical tools to reduce waste and variability.

Parinaz Sekechi is a learning and development professional with extensive experience working with diverse and global environments. As a learning consultant in Alcatel-Lucent University, she facilitates the analysis of the gap between the current state and desired state of employee learning, specifically Emerging and Critical Talent, and People Managers, to provide a learning solution that's aligned with the needs of the business.

Byron Gilliam has been trading securities markets for 20 years, including stints at Citigroup and UniCredit. He began his trading career in

Frankfurt, Germany, and subsequently traded out of London, Paris, and New York. Byron has traded U.S., European, and emerging market equities, equity derivatives and currencies on both a proprietary and customer basis. Byron's trading roles have included three years on a proprietary desk (where he achieved double digit returns each year), a time on an Equity Capital Markets desk where he bid for and unwound large block transactions for customers, and his current role as head of U.S. trading for Olivetree Securities.

Phil Hall is a preeminent vocal coach and voice teacher for musical theater. On Broadway, he conducted *Play Me a Country Song* and assistant conducted the revival of *Mame* starring Angela Lansbury. He is an accomplished pianist, accompanist, and published arranger. He composed *Dr. Jekyll and Mr. Hyde*, which was performed at Paper Mill Playhouse, Kansas City Starlight, North Shore Music Theater, and Santa Barbara Civic Light Opera. He wrote the book, music, and lyrics to *Matthew Passion* (see *www.matthewpassion.com*).

Ron Raines has had a long and illustrious international career that spans the worlds of musical theater, opera, cabaret, classical music, and television. He was a three-time Emmy and Soap Opera Digest Award nominee for his role as the villain Alan Spaulding on CBS's longest running daytime drama *Guiding Light* and has starred on Broadway in shows such as *Chicago*, *Newsies*, *Follies* (Tony nomination), and *Annie*. He has soloed with more than 50 major American and international orchestras. He lives in New York City with his wife and daughter.

Martin Samual works in film, television, and theater all over the world. His credits include *Aida* on Broadway, the U.S. tour of *Joseph and the Amazing Technicolor Dreamcoat*, the first national tour of *Dirty Rotten Scoundrels*, the Oscar-winning film *Chicago*, the TV film *Once Upon a Mattress* (with Carol Burnett), *One Life to Live*, and more. He lives in New York City.

Riley Nelson is currently a junior at the Latin School of Chicago, with PSAT scores placing him in the 99th percentile of his peers in all categories nationwide. He has peddled everything from pencils to laser pointers and jewelry to his classmates before discovering Bitcoin two years ago. He is now president of Acoin LLC, a start up holdings company in the digital currency space.

Bud Martin, executive director, Delaware Theatre Company, is a former teacher and financier. He has three children and six grandchildren and lives with his wife on a horse farm (his other dream come true) in Southern Chester County, Pennsylvania.

Tom Blakey, a longtime volunteer at the National WWII Museum in New Orleans, was a combat veteran and paratrooper with the U.S. Army Double A "All American, 82nd Airborne." He jumped on the morning of June 6, 1944, behind the Nazi lines in Normandy. His combat service stretched from France to Holland, including action in the surprise German offensive in the Ardennes Forest known as the Battle of the Bulge. Blakey is also an active member of the Museum's Speakers Bureau. He travels across the region to speak with schools, senior and community centers, and other groups about his war experiences. He recently returned to Normandy for the 70th Anniversary of the D-Day Invasion.

Known as "The Pope of Wargaming," **Richard Berg** has over 150 published games, including Terrible Swift Sword and SPQR. He is a 13-time winner of the Industry Award for Best Game Design. His other awards include: GAMA Hall of Fame, 1993; Charles Roberts Award for Lifetime Achievement in Simulation Design, 1990; and the Bloomgren/Hamilton Memorial Award for Lifetime Achievement in 2003.

Linda Moshier is a gardener, singer, wife, and mom to three fluffy Lhasa's. Her adventures in homesteading began after receiving a Permaculture Design Certification with wildcrafter Michael Pilarski and Austrian Sepp Holtzer. She traveled internationally as a USO entertainer and continues in New York City performing the American Songbook. Linda is currently writing a book entitled *Ideas From the Bench*, a collection of essays on life and gardening as told from her daily sitting spot.

Francine LaSala has written nonfiction on every topic imaginable, from circus freaks to sex, and edited bestselling authors of all genres. She is the author of novels *Rita Hayworth's Shoes* and *The Girl, The Gold Tooth & Everything*, co-editor and publisher of the short story anthology *A Kind of Mad Courage*, and the creator of the "Joy Jar" Project. She lives with her husband and two daughters in New York.

Index

About the Author

A former television producer, journalist, and professional spokesperson, **Karen E. Berg** is a sought-after motivational speaker, executive coach, and communications trainer. A popular on-camera communication coach for Fortune 500 companies' educational Websites, Karen has been a lecturer on communication issues for the Center for Disease Control (CDC), Department of Defense, Albert Einstein College of Medicine, Wharton School of Business, New York University, Yale University, Semmelweis University in Budapest, and CETRA in Taipei. As CEO of CommCore Strategies, Karen has worked with hundreds of C-Suite leaders and thousands of subject matter experts to prepare them for important events, including media interviews, crisis communications, shareholders meetings, and management and peer-to-peer presentations. She has also helped thousands of people across all industries communicate messages on controversial issues, including assisting spokespeople at the global pharmaceutical firm Johnson & Johnson during the Tylenol crisis.